CONTENDING FOR THE FAITH

E. J. Poole-Connor
A 'prophet' amidst the sweeping changes
in English evangelicalism

DAVID G. FOUNTAIN

THE WAKEMAN TRUST, LONDON

Originally entitled:
E. J. POOLE-CONNOR, 'Contender for the Faith'
© David G. Fountain, 1966

New, abridged and revised edition 2005 entitled:
CONTENDING FOR THE FAITH, E. J. Poole-Connor
A 'prophet' amidst the sweeping changes in English evangelicalism

THE WAKEMAN TRUST
(UK Registered Charity)

Website: www.wakemantrust.org

UK Registered Office
38 Walcot Square
London SE11 4TZ

US Office
300 Artino Drive
Oberlin, OH 44074-1263

ISBN 1 870855 32 9

Cover design by Andrew Owen
Cover image of E. J. Poole-Connor courtesy of the Bodleian Library, Oxford

Printed by Stephens & George, Merthyr Tydfil, UK

CONTENDING FOR THE FAITH

Foreword to the Original Work
by Dr D. Martyn Lloyd-Jones

I HAVE MUCH enjoyed reading this account of the life and doings of my friend. What marks E. J. Poole-Connor out and makes him worthy of our attention is his work and thinking in connection with the leading problem of our age – the question of the nature of the Christian church, and especially the relationship of the evangelical Christian to that problem. His excellent book *Evangelicalism in England* showed his grasp and understanding of that problem in a masterly manner.

Here, we have not only the essence of that history judiciously selected and presented, but also the part which he himself played in the making of that history in the present century, and particularly in connection with the formation of the Fellowship of Independent Evangelical Churches.

David Fountain has produced a perfect blend of history and doctrine which is most instructive and thought-provoking. The reading of this book cannot but clarify the thinking of all who are deeply concerned about evangelical witness at the present time and in the years that lie ahead. I therefore strongly and heartily recommend it to all and pray that God may bless it and use it.

D. M. LLOYD-JONES

Westminster Chapel
February, 1966

Contents

Introduction
A Unique Life Spanning
Great Changes in the Churches

E DWARD Joshua Poole-Connor was God's remarkable gift to His people during a troubled and confused time, and his convictions have a very valuable application in our own day. When I began the task of writing this biography, I soon discovered that there was virtually nothing written from an evangelical stand-point about the period of history in which Poole-Connor lived (1872-1962) – once described as 'a period without parallel in human history, during which the church was devastated by error of every kind, Nonconformity lost its power, and once full chapels were found desolate and deserted . . .'

This encouraged me to believe there would be great interest in the historical background of this dramatic period of change. The present volume, therefore, traces the life of E. J. Poole-Connor, and his reaction to the major events in the evangelical world during the collapse of English Nonconformity.

Poole-Connor himself, through his writings, provided so much material, both historical and personal, that it seemed only right to quote often from him, which also serves to illustrate his powerful writing gift. In style this book follows very closely Poole-Connor's own method. His works were for serious Christians who were prepared to go into matters and to face up to facts, and I have found myself following his methods and approach.

Though I knew Poole-Connor personally, I certainly could not claim a deep acquaintance with him, and though history was the speciality of my undergraduate days, the last hundred years seemed, from the spiritual point of view, an uncharted continent. However, in the providence of God, I was given more help than I could have dreamed of. A close friend of Poole-Connor, George Fromow, surprised me by presenting me with his collection of practically all the articles the former had written during his lifetime. A former Treasurer of the Talbot Tabernacle, London, likewise surprised me with an unexpected store of information, having kept a record of everything of importance that took place during the two periods Mr Poole-Connor was minister there, including all the monthly *Tabernacle Notes*. My most important source of information was Mrs Edith Poole-Connor, whose memory was still very clear. When I had my last interview with her shortly before her death, I was left with the feeling that I had received all the information that I needed. Others also supplied me with much material.

E. J. Poole-Connor, whom God called home 40 years ago, has given us a challenging role model, both in his defence of the faith, and in his pastoral life. We, sadly, lack such role models today and do well to look again at his life. God uses examples but, alas, there are so few who have the consistency and genuineness of this pastor, educator and writer. It must be conceded that some aspects of his view of evangelical unity must be looked at again in the light of unfolding events since his lifetime. Weaknesses in his thinking need to be considered in the light of the development of the body of

churches he founded. But what was outstanding was his prepared-
ness to do everything within his power to glorify God in the
extension of His kingdom.

He was, indeed, a 'contender for the faith', a feature that stands
out above everything else in his life. It is also clear that he was prepared to contend even when virtually alone, and to do so in a
gracious and biblical fashion.

DAVID G. FOUNTAIN

Sholing, Southampton
2004

Glossary of Terms

for a new generation of readers who may be unfamiliar with these words, once in common use in churches

ANGLICAN: Belonging to the Church of England.

BAPTIST: Holding that baptism is for believers only, by immersion, and that individual congregations are self-governing. (Baptists arose in the UK in the 17th century. In the 19th century the majority were grouped into one totally evangelical denomination, the Baptist Union, but this now has very few evangelicals. Most evangelical Baptists are now independent.)

CONGREGATIONALIST: Holding that individual congregations are self-governing, and practising infant baptism. (The Congregational Union in Britain merged with English Presbyterians in 1967 to become the United Reformed Church. Evangelicals are now rare.)

DISSENTER: A person not part of the Church of England and therefore free from its control. The main dissenting denominations in England were the Baptists, the Congregationalists and the Methodists. (Means the same as Nonconformist.)

HIGHER CRITICISM: Technically this is the study of a Bible text to determine its authorship, time of writing, literary structure and sense. However, the real character of higher criticism is much worse than this. It is the view that scholarship may speculate freely which texts are authentic and correct, and which should be seen as myth rather than history. Higher criticism rejects the divine inspiration and infallibility of the Bible.

LIBERAL: Free from, and not bound by, the total authority of the Bible, believing that religion must advance with the changing views of society. Theological liberals are in favour of higher criticism.

METHODIST: The second largest group of churches in England, begun by the Wesleys at the Great Awakening of the 18th century. In the 1900s they gradually became one denomination. There are now very few evangelicals.

MODERNIST: Same as liberal; believing that reason and modern thought carry greater weight than the Bible.

NONCONFORMIST: Same as Dissenter; a church or person not part of the Church of England and free from its control.

PROTESTANT: Any church or person in favour of the Reformation as opposed to the Roman Catholic Church. All evangelicals are Protestants.

[Other terms little used today are defined in footnotes through the book.]

1

Getting to Know the Man

WHO WAS THE man who so discerningly put his finger on the wrong turnings of British church life, and who powerfully urged corrective remedies? We surely like to know the stature and characteristics of eyewitnesses and interpreters of major events. We noted in the introduction that Edward Joshua Poole-Connor's life (1872-1962) spanned probably the most disastrous period of church history this country has ever known, yet throughout that long and dismal time his own testimony shone brightly and clearly. Three characteristics marked him out: his godliness, his great variety of talents, and the discerning convictions that led to his magnificent defence of the faith.

Throughout life his saintliness made a deep impression on others. From the time when his headmaster was impressed by the influence he had on other children, until the day of his death, testimonies survive of his practical godliness. Some 'contenders' are almost natural fighters, but Poole-Connor was richly endowed with kindliness and

thoughtfulness, and whenever he was provoked and tried, grace prevailed. At his memorial service many paid tribute to his outstanding
patience and self-control. He displayed a consistency throughout his
long life, arising from his conscientious policy of learning and self-
improvement as a minister. He was one, for example, who knew
how to promote calm reflection and agreement. His keenness to
develop this quality is seen in his book *Evangelical Unity*. He was
most interested in the report of the meeting during which the Evangelical Alliance was formed in 1846. It was for him, as he tells us, the
'inner story' of the movement, 'full of instruction for the reader', an
object lesson, teaching *how* to pour oil on troubled waters, and learn
spiritual and wise leadership.

'We are taught,' he wrote, 'that a movement of the Holy Spirit
may yet be orderly and subject to rule. We observe the importance
of a competent Chairman. We are taught that there are occasions
in a business meeting when a few minutes given to prayer is of the
utmost value. We see where it is wise to yield, and where to be firm.
We learn that it is sometimes well to remit a matter to a sub-
committee. Any man who is responsible for a project which he
believes to be of God, yet in which it is necessary to carry with him
brethren of varying temperament and outlook, will find here much
to enlighten him. Further, we are shown the means by which the evil
one may be permitted to frustrate the hopes and purposes of the
people of God . . . If any man desires to learn how a vessel sailing
through calm seas and under blue skies may suddenly strike a hidden rock, let him read this cautionary report, and be warned afresh
against the "wiles of the devil".' Poole-Connor was just such a
learner.

It is sometimes the case that the friends of one who has passed on
to be with Christ are inclined to exaggerate the merits of their
friend, and to pass over his faults. This writer has seen a wealth of
material, including private correspondence, which shows beyond

doubt that Poole-Connor was a man who displayed a graciousness, kindness and humility amidst most testing circumstances and provocations. This calm poise and balance was one of his most remarkable qualities. The writer remembers, some fifty years ago, putting the question to him, 'What advice would you give to a young minister?' The answer, so characteristic of him, was, 'Be patient.'

Some considered him rather cold and remote, and although at times he gave this impression, it was not the case with him. It was perfectly natural for him to be reserved, being a man of pronounced personal discipline. There was certainly a godly seriousness about him. His very unwillingness to be an exhibitionist in an age when this was so common led some to underestimate his great worth. He was no opportunist, and was prepared, if need be, to be regarded as of little consequence for the sake of being consistent and faithful. He frequently found himself having to take a major step of faith.

While there was a seriousness about him, there was also humour and subtle wit permeating his writings. He had a gentle manner of repartee, and his pleasure in amusing children was infectious. In his early days of promoting the Fellowship of Independent Evangelical Churches his 'open letters' were delightful in their informality and humour. He possessed great skill as a story-teller, and his fund of anecdotes seemed inexhaustible, especially as he knew intimately some of the great evangelical leaders of earlier days, and his stories of Dr Tom Barnardo and others were an education in themselves.

What Dr Samuel Johnson said of John Wesley could be said of Poole-Connor also – 'I could talk with him all day and all night too. I found in him an habitual gaiety of heart. He is the most perfect specimen of moral happiness I ever saw. In Wesley's speech and temper I discovered more to teach me what a Heaven upon earth is like than all I have elsewhere seen or heard or read, except in the sacred volume.' A comparison with Wesley could well be pursued in other departments of life when one remembers Poole-Connor's longevity, great ability and organising skill.

There are, sad to say, 'great men' who are like some great paintings – seen at their best from a distance. If you look closely at them there is little order or beauty. This was not the case with Poole-Connor. Godliness, true godliness, was his outstanding characteristic.

Poole-Connor was not only a decided man of God, but a person of great gifts and varied ability. In these days gifts and popularity are generally equated, though they are seldom found together when accompanied by sincerity and faithfulness. He would probably have made a bad salesman, advertising agent or comedian, but nevertheless possessed such a variety of gifts that he could have done exceptionally well in a number of other spheres. He possessed a love of beauty, and was himself artistic. In early years he worked as a professional builder for a time, and on one occasion built his own house. He was endowed with a business capacity which he used to good effect in the conduct of the material side of the affairs of churches and societies.

Poole-Connor was both a natural and an industrious scholar, being greatly helped by a remarkable memory. His writings are strewn with quotations that reveal his love of literature and his vast reading. He thought logically and expressed himself clearly, not only in print, but from the pulpit. It was always a pleasure to listen to the choiceness of his diction.

In spiritual gifts he excelled, the greatest of these being his ability to expound the Scriptures, and his pastoral wisdom. Penetrating and definite in interpretation, he was always courteous to the views of others, illustrated by his favourite opening phrase: 'As I understand the Scripture . . .'

This God-sent leader knew particularly well how to lead, inspire, and sometimes contain others in difficult situations. As a Chairman, his ability was renowned. As Editor of the *Bible League Quarterly* he gave a lead and a sense of direction to bewildered Christians on many issues. As a prominent writer and church leader, his statesmanship and almost prophetic utterances were remarkable.

There was one particular gift that Poole-Connor considered he did not have – the gift of an evangelist. However, it speaks well of his humility and his love for souls that he willingly sought to reach men, women and children with the Gospel. His North Sea ministry brought him into contact with ill-educated seamen, and his pastorates also provided him with many occasions for evangelistic enterprise. At Talbot Tabernacle in London, though he addressed hundreds week by week, he was burdened for the thousands outside, organising a massive Sunday School of a thousand youngsters, and evangelising the entire district by monthly tracts and local congregational visitation.

We have observed that Poole-Connor lived during a period of unparalleled spiritual decline in the United Kingdom. Clearly, God raised him up to act as a watchman in such times, and he proved faithful to his calling. In the clearest way he focused minds on the spiritual collapse going on around him, while others, particularly evangelical leaders, who should have known, were either oblivious to it, or chose to do nothing about it and kept silent. In this whole matter he was inspired by the conduct of C. H. Spurgeon during the Down-Grade Controversy.

2

Forming Discernment

'I WAS BORN twelve years after the revival of 1860, because although it commenced in 1858, it was perhaps at its peak in the year 1860. I was born into a Christian family, and while the tide was rapidly receding, I was still conscious as I became old enough to think about these things, that there was a power still in the Christian churches and in Christian homes, that has long since disappeared.' So spoke Poole-Connor on a memorable occasion while dealing with the subject of 'revival'. He heard C. H. Spurgeon, Hudson Taylor and many others, and witnessed a period of great change not only in the physical world round about him, but in the spiritual life of the churches.

A glance at his childhood provides a precious insight into the strong evangelicalism of those days. He came from a godly home where he was encouraged to read the story of the pilgrimage of God's people in Britain, and he loved to read and speak about the great heroes of the faith and the triumphs of the Gospel. From the time when, at the age of eighteen, as local Secretary of the Calvinistic Protestant Union, he delivered lectures on church history in a schoolroom near his home, until sixty years later when he wrote his brilliant sweep of church history entitled, *Evangelicalism in England*, the theme absorbed him fully.

He described his family background in these words: 'Evangelical Protestantism has been ingrained in our family for many generations. Our ancestors were members of the Irish Roman Catholic clan of the O'Connors, and when one of them was converted to simple faith in Christ his life was endangered; but it was spared on condition that he left Ireland and omitted the prefix "O" from his name, thereby renouncing all clan claims and privileges. One of his descendants (my grandfather) married a godly English lady, a Miss Poole, who so endeared herself to her numerous family that they grafted her maiden name onto their own; thus the compound cognomen came into existence. My beloved father, who was a deacon of the Calvinistic Independent church in Hackney, a most saintly man, early trained me in the tenets and history of Protestantism.'

As a child he attended Trinity Chapel, Hackney, with his family. This community of Christians not only expressed the very best that was to be found in 19th-century English Nonconformity, but retained it at a time when the Free Churches were rapidly changing.

Poole-Connor gives us a brief account of his early church life in *Evangelical Unity*: 'I had the inestimable privilege of being born into a godly household; and my earliest recollections are of the large and stately place of worship which my parents were accustomed to attend, and to which they took their children. It was the home of an influential community, usually regarded as Calvinistic Independents, a branch of the Congregational body; but it was, in fact, an Independent church in the more strict sense of the term. It was founded by Thomas Hughes, MA, a former clergyman of the

Church of England who, for reasons unknown to me, had seceded and established a separate congregation. He was a preacher of great powers, and had a very numerous following. He was of Welsh nationality, and when greatly moved in prayer or public ministry he would fall into the musical semi-chant which is known amongst his countrymen as the "hwyl". His labours resulted in the conversion of large numbers, although mainly directed to the edification of believers. He dwelt much upon the theme of union with Christ and with the invisible church . . . The sense of the presence of God, my father told me, was often overpowering. I was thus born and cradled in a non-sectarian atmosphere.'

We learn from the *Bible League Quarterly* that he was 'nurtured on the writings of the Puritans'. In *Evangelical Unity* he wrote: 'As I grew older I came to perceive that while I was greatly blessed in both my parents, my father in particular was a man of peculiar sanctity of character, who all his life walked with God. He never spoke in public, except in the exercise of his great gift of prayer. He would generally pray at length in the church prayer meetings – they all did in those days, sometimes taking as long as twenty or twenty-five minutes – but when my father was so engaged time to me seemed to stand still. I can remember that occasionally when I thought he was about to close, I would say under my breath, "Go on, father dear! Don't leave off yet." Is it to be wondered that such a parent should leave a deep and lifelong impression upon his son?'

It was in such a spiritual environment, at home and at the house of God, that Poole-Connor grew up. The Lord's Day was for him the happiest day of the week. Many of that time had like privileges, but few appreciated them. As a child he was delicate and not expected to live. Before he was born three girls and one boy had died, and the doctors feared that he would not survive. He was allowed to do what he wanted, since it was thought would not have long in this world, but by the age of eight he was strong. He had one sister, seven years younger than he, who was healthy from her birth.

He and his future wife, Edith Ford (who was a little older than he), knew each other at an early age. They lived in the same area, and he used to play regularly with her younger brother and sister in their large garden. He went to the same school as her two elder brothers, and when he was only twelve he was the means of converting one of them. He tells us that from his earliest childhood he had been taught to trust in the Saviour. His first convert would later be pastor of a church at Brentwood, near London, for twenty years.

His father was formerly an artist of considerable skill, but his work so greatly absorbed his mind that he decided to become a builder and decorator. He started a business and employed several men. Poole-Connor himself might have taken up painting if he had not felt a strong longing to go into the ministry. Poole-Connor's natural skill can be seen in the paintings of seamen and sea scenes which he made during a period as a missionary with the North Sea fishing fleet. His interest in art also came out in his writings.

When Poole-Connor was thirteen his father became very ill, and remained so for a considerable time, with the result that the son was forced to leave the private school he attended. When the headmaster heard of it he was deeply concerned, and so anxious that this lad should continue at school that he offered to pay the fees if it was a question of money. He said to his father, 'He has such a good influence on the other boys.' But Poole-Connor had to leave and take over his father's business. At thirteen he was like a man, his wife recalled later. He taught a Sunday School class, with several of his pupils older than himself.

It must have seemed very hard to him that he should have had an interrupted education, but it was a wise providence that ordained it so, for it left him with an unusually intense desire to learn, which he never lost. When his father died he spent the little sum left to him in order to make up what he had lacked. He wanted to go to college, and later attended lectures at London University, using his precious savings in this way. Unlike some who, having enjoyed the privileges of a lengthy education, lose the desire for intensive study, he was a deeply disciplined student till the last day of his life. He could not fall into the snare of relying on an academic reputation, but God had endowed him with a remarkable memory and a great love of reading. In truth, Poole-Connor was an entirely natural scholar. The certainty of his convictions, and the authority with which he spoke, were naturally associated with the way he arrived at his views, for he had to find out for himself.

At the age of fifteen he was admitted to the membership of Trinity Chapel, Hackney. He would also attend the great Protestant gatherings at the old Exeter Hall. A Baptist minister from Harringay took an interest in him and encouraged him in his budding desire to enter the ministry, and at the age of eighteen he preached his 'trial' sermon, subsequently studying for the ministry under the Harringay minister. While still eighteen he took on the oversight of a little church in South Hackney for a year; an experience that taught him much. He was introduced to Dr James Spurgeon, C. H. Spurgeon's brother, with a view to his entering the 'Pastors' College' (as it was then known), but he chose instead to accept a call to the oversight of the Aldershot Baptist Church, coupled with a chaplaincy of Baptists in the army garrison there. This he did at the age of twenty-one.

While Poole-Connor was growing up and preparing himself for the ministry, great changes were taking place round about him. He could not possibly grasp the seriousness of them at the time, but he witnessed many of them at first hand, and in later years analysed them, and frequently referred to them.

3
The Glorious Heritage of the Free Churches

FOR MANY Poole-Connor was a link with the late-Victorian era, but he was more than a Victorian. He seemed to epitomise all that was best in the English Free Churches[*] of the first half of the 19th century. This was another world spiritually, a world rich in its appreciation of the Word of God. The reason he could describe so well the Nonconformist heritage in his books was because of his early environment, extensive reading and deep appreciation of the privileges that were his.

The Hackney chapel of his upbringing had retained its orthodoxy even when fundamental doctrines expressed in the great confessions began to be disregarded. It remained firmly autonomous as the great movements towards denominational centralisation threatened the strong allegiance to local church government in the Free

---

[*]Free Churches: another term for Nonconformist churches, not part of the Church of England.

Churches. It had pastors who had left the Church of England and were therefore moving in the very opposite direction to the trends among the denominations. In short, Trinity Chapel still retained the precious Nonconformist heritage of the first half of the 19th century during the second half. Poole-Connor breathed that atmosphere and later communicated it to his hearers and readers, adding a freshness and a vital modern application. In order to understand the heritage he enjoyed, and the phenomenal changes that later took place, it is vital to know something of the condition of the Free Churches in the first half of the 19th century.

Heresy was ever at hand, but made little progress until after 1860. The scripturality and orthodoxy of the churches were owned and blessed by God in that great miracle known as the 1859 Revival, when it is believed that somewhere near a million people were added to the kingdom of God. It is not only absorbing but strictly relevant for us to begin our history by considering the state of our fathers in the faith in the early 19th century, for it brings us face to face with the astonishing change that took place in so short a time. The contrast between then and now is most marked.

In his book, *The Apostasy of English Nonconformity*, when dealing with the 'doctrinal belief of earlier Nonconformists', Poole-Connor tells us that 'until a comparatively *recent* period *[he wrote these words in 1933]* the doctrines of Nonconformists were those of the Puritans; and upon the proclamation of them the divine blessing manifestly rested.' The evidence bears this out plainly. Another book, *Evangelical Unity*, devotes a chapter to the 'Evangelical Alliance', showing that during the 1840s and 1850s evangelicals were fully convinced and agreed on the fundamentals of the faith. The churches were strongly Protestant and evangelical, and opposed to modernism or theological liberalism.

The seeds of heresy may well have been in the hearts of many, but in 1846 there were still few outward signs. There was a wonderful

unity on the great fundamentals of the faith among the Noncon-
formist denominations. They were nearly all true evangelicals. John
Angell James, a typically loyal evangelical, led the fray both against
Rome and the high-church party in the Church of England,* and the
so-called 'German error' (later called modernism). In 1850, when
Pope Pius IX re-established Roman Catholic bishops in England,
Dr John Morison expressed the attitude of most Congregationalists:
'Everyone not judicially blind sees that the Tractarians are the osten-
sible allies of the "man of sin".'[1]

The historian Tudur Jones tells us, 'The first intimation that the
older orthodoxy was being challenged was the appearance of
Edward White's *Life of Christ* in 1846.'[2] White denied the immortality of the soul, but as yet he received little open support. The
Evangelical Magazine attacked it as a 'great and dangerous heresy',
and he was virtually excluded from the Nonconformist pulpits of
the land. A little later, in 1855, a storm of controversy broke out
over a book of religious poetry by the Congregationalist minister,
Thomas Toke Lynch. It was condemned because it contained 'not
one particle of vital religion or evangelical piety'. Watchdogs were
waiting for the first signs of modernism. Dr John Campbell, Pastor
of Whitefield's Tabernacle, London, and a close friend of Spurgeon,
vigorously attacked Lynch, and at the same time made this remarkable assessment of the spiritual condition of the times:

'We hesitate not to assert that at no period of our country's history
was the Dissenting pulpit ever more thoroughly, more unequivocally evangelical than at the present hour. We know what we say and
whereof we affirm. A greater mistake could not be committed than
to identify the London Dissenting Ministry with the theology of

---

*The high-church party, also known as the Tractarians, were fervently active in
the Church of England, becoming famous for ninety bulky pamphlets called
Tracts for the Times, by leading pro-Catholic churchmen.

The Rivulet [the name given to Lynch's volume]; almost to a man, that theology – such as it is, for it is no theology at all – is to them an object of contempt and condemnation. There is not among them, we believe, a man who would not stand by the most searching theological examination . . .'[3]

There was a growing interest in modernism, but for at least another twenty years it was expedient for sympathising ministers to keep their opinions to themselves.

Tudur Jones gives us helpful guidance as we look for further evidence of prevailing soundness among Nonconformists in the first half of the 19th century. He writes: 'For Congregationalists, as for other Protestants, the Bible had always held a unique place in their affections as the infallible authority to which Christians must defer. Any re-evaluation of its nature and infallibility would of necessity have far-reaching repercussions over the whole of religious and moral life. The second half of the 19th century saw precisely such a re-evaluation.'[4]

Despite the soundness in theology, there is no doubt there was spiritual lethargy, provoking the comment by John Angell James in 1851: 'The state of religion in our country is low. I do not think I ever preached with less saving results since I was a minister and this is the case with most others. It is a general complaint.' The most striking illustration of the coldness of many Nonconformists is to be found in the reception C. H. Spurgeon received when he began his ministry in London in 1854. Baptist historian Thomas Armitage writes: 'He possessed some youthful eccentricities which to the eyes of many staid folk savoured of boldness and self-conceit. On this plea every sort of indecent attack was made upon him; the writer well remembers the time when but two or three ministers in London treated him with common respect, to say nothing of Christian courtesy; but God was with him and that was enough.'

However, while there was a growing spiritual sluggishness and complacency, the Truth still had a firm root. It was because evangelicalism held universal sway among Nonconformists that the Great Awakening of 1859 reached unprecedented proportions. The large dissenting denominations which had been in existence for two hundred years after separating from the Church of England were unquestionably sound in doctrine.

English Nonconformists of the early 19th century not only had a firm hold on the fundamentals of the faith, but a very clearly defined view of the church. Presbyterians were few and scattered, coming from Scotland in the main (the English Presbyterians having turned Unitarian[*] in the previous century). Nonconformists saw the local congregation as a spiritual family unit. Hale White describes the Congregational church in Bedford thus: 'The old meeting-house held about 700 people and was filled every Sunday. It was not the gifts of the minister, certainly after the days of my early childhood, which kept such a congregation steady.'[5] 'Independency was far from an individualism that finds in the church chiefly a personal relation to the pastor. Nonconformists went to the meeting to find God among His saints . . . Their concern to make the boundaries of the visible and invisible church coincide was expressed in the conception of the church as a company of Christians gathered from the world, with its discipline to ensure that so far as possible non-Christians were kept out [of the membership, that is], and its toleration of minor differences to make equally sure that all Christians were allowed in.'[6]

They believed – 'The visible church shall consist, as far as wisdom and vigilance can secure such a result, of those who are members of the church invisible.'[7] This is the principle that churches should only admit into membership people who are truly converted, as opposed to the Anglican conception that embraces all the people who live in

---

[*]Unitarians deny the doctrine of the Trinity.

the parish, whether they seem to be converted or not.

It is true that the Independents or Congregationalists became lax about discipline and would in time succumb to modernism, but that was not due to their doctrine of the church. John Stoughton admitted that a perfect purity of fellowship could never be obtained, but added: 'This is no reason why such purity as is obtainable should not be wisely and strenuously aimed at.' Care to preserve evangelical doctrines was also expressed by safeguards in the trust-deeds of chapels: 'The buildings used for Nonconformist worship were commonly provided with trust-deeds limiting their use to pastors who shall hold, teach, preach, and maintain the doctrines set forth in the schedule hereto.'[8]

Local churches respected this: 'The kind of unity we maintain, and which exists between all the Congregational churches in this town, is very real. If one church excommunicates a member, no other church will receive him into fellowship without conference with the church from which he was expelled. It would be a grave offence to admit a man into one church after he had been expelled from another, until he had shown adequate penitence for his offence.'[9]

It was not their doctrine of the church that laid Nonconformists open to decline. It was when they rejected the *Gospel itself* that it became natural for them to open their doors to heretics and unbelievers.

In 1851 a census was taken in England and Wales of those who attended church or chapel. About a third of the population attended regularly, this section being equally divided between Anglican and Nonconformist, the latter having slightly more places of worship. With the Great Awakening to come in 1859, and many social disabilities to be removed, Nonconformity was to have a vast influence in the life of the country. However, as the churches became more 'influential' within society they began to drift away from their spiritual moorings.

The social background of this period is important, for it is hard to appreciate how the majority of people lived in the mid-19th century. The first Public Health Act dates from 1848. It resulted from the frequent cholera epidemics, and from the efforts of one of the Poor Law Commissioners who had come to realise the facts, revealing physical suffering and moral disorder amongst the cellar populations of the working people of Liverpool, Manchester and Leeds, and in large portions of the Metropolis. The main principle of the reforming Act of 1848 was *permission* rather than compulsion to act, and it was not properly carried out by the municipalities for another twenty years. The great social changes of the Victorian era can be attributed largely to the influence of the godly, as salt upon the corrupt body of society. G. M. Trevelyan sets the scene:

'The mass of unregarded humanity in the factories and mines were as yet without any social services or amusements of a modern kind to compensate for the lost amenities and traditions of country life. They were wholly uncared for by church or State; no Lady Bountiful visited them with blankets and advice; no one but the Nonconformist minister was their friend; they had no luxury but drink, no one to talk to but one another, hardly any subject but their grievances. Naturally they were tinder to the flame of agitation.

'They had no interest or hope in life but evangelical religion or radical politics. Sometimes the two went together, for many Nonconformist preachers themselves imbibed and imparted radical doctrines. But the political conservatism with which the Wesleyan movement had started was not yet exhausted, and acted as a restraining element. The power of evangelical religion was the chief influence that prevented our country from starting along the path of revolutionary violence during this period of economic chaos and social neglect.'[10]

As a result of all this, the influence of the Gospel was very widespread among the lower classes. Though much was lacking in the organised education of that age as compared with our own, very many people of all classes knew the Bible with real familiarity.

Evangelicals within the Church of England were not confined to the lower classes. During the first thirty years of the 19th century many changes in habits of life and thought were due to the steady infiltration of evangelical religion into all classes of society, not excepting the highest; it was a movement that spread from below upwards. This was due not only to the godliness of Nonconformists, but the influential evangelical party of the Church of England, which now had a lodging place inside the State church. Charles Simeon exerted a great influence. 'Had it not been for Simeon, the evangelical clergy would have continued to drift into Dissent.'[11] With the exception of Charles Simeon and Isaac Milner of Cambridge, the leading 'Saints' (as the evangelicals were popularly called) were laymen – Wilberforce, the Buxtons and the 'Clapham Sect'. The strongest type of English gentlemen in the new era were often evangelical. The army knew them with respect, and India with gratitude. Through families like the Stephens, their influence on Downing Street, the permanent Civil Service and the colonial administration constantly increased during the first forty years of the century.

A striking illustration of this is to be found in the case of the committee of the Commons set up to enquire into the 'aborigines question' for South Africa, at the request of a prominent evangelical. It recommended that, 'Well matured schemes for advancing social and political improvement were to be combined with their moral and *religious* improvement.'

Historian Keith Feiling calls the Victorian age a 'golden age', and says that the British were more 'religious' at this age than at any date since the Commonwealth. The fate of many Governments and composition of many Cabinets was determined by religious causes. Feiling pays this tribute to the now-disparaged Victorian era: 'Few civilizations have left such enduring spiritual monuments, wielded such political power or expanded in such rapid material progress as that of Great Britain in the mid-Victorian age.'[12] But note, he refers to the 'mid-Victorian age'. After 1840 Anglican evangelicals began to decline in numbers and influence. The 1859 Revival centred on Nonconformity rather than the Church of England, for the latter was yielding to Catholic Tractarianism. The Prime Minister, Lord John Russell, wrote to the Bishop of Durham (1850) complaining that, 'Clergymen of our own church who have subscribed to the 39 Articles and acknowledged in explicit terms the Queen's supremacy, have been the most forward in leading their flocks "step by step to the very verge of the precipice".' The Anglican evangelicals reached the height of their influence early in the century, but it was ebbing away before the 1850s.

The 1859 Revival was conspicuous mostly for its proportions. Dr Edwin Orr, in his book *The Second Evangelical Awakening*, calculates that around one million souls were added to the kingdom, and his figure may be regarded as reasonably authentic. Much has been written about this wonderful visit of divine grace which is easily accessible today.

Ulster, Wales and Scotland experienced powerful movements of the Spirit in 1859, and parts of England were also affected. C. H. Spurgeon's Metropolitan Tabernacle, for example, was greatly blessed through the Revival. The power of God was so great that this awakening continued for many years. It was preceded by a great prayer movement, and followed by great effectiveness in the ministry of God's servants. Poole-Connor was keenly aware of the difference between the effectiveness of the ministry in churches generally through the time of his youth, and subsequently.

After the 1859 Revival an impetus was given to the modern missionary movement that had begun around 1815. This, at first, had been slow, hard, pioneering work, but soon multitudes of missionary recruits heartened those pioneers in their toil. The 19th century was certainly the century of missionary expansion; but we refer to it here only because it was a proof of the genuineness of the 1859 Revival. Many societies were formed for the spread of the Gospel abroad and at home. It was a truly great revival, the greatest in extensiveness, and it was followed by lasting fruit.

Ominously, alongside that great revival came the publication of the first of a number of books that undermined the message of the Bible, Darwin's *The Origin of Species* being the first and most influential of these. Darwin's theory of evolution was applied to every aspect of the life of man, and had a profound effect upon Old Testament studies, placing them within an evolutionary framework. This encouraged the radical re-dating of Bible books (already begun by the so-called 'higher critics'). The supernatural character of biblical religion came, gradually at first, to be denied, and Israel's history came to be seen as a natural and evolutionary development of the thought and practice of a particularly religious people.

With the second half of the 19th century Nonconformist churches became more 'respectable', and ideas that were intellectually acceptable in society began to find a home within them. The character of Nonconformist churches underwent a change as the 'local church family' aspect gave way to the massed congregation.

'To accommodate the great congregations the meeting-houses were often pulled down to make way for large edifices "in the Gothic style" that should accommodate four-figure congregations in crowded pews, and should be in their outward architecture eloquent of the ambition and success of Dissent. The worst aspect of all this was the tendency to treat the preacher much in the same fashion as the film-actor is now treated, and to regard public worship as something like a respectable public entertainment.'[13]

It was inevitable that this would begin to lead to greater pretentiousness and less personal earnestness in the conduct of public worship. In the November 1865 issue of *The Sword and the Trowel*, the monthly magazine published by Spurgeon at the Metropolitan Tabernacle, an article appeared on forms of prayer, which stated, 'There is a growing tendency in Dissenting churches to mimic the Church of England.'

Even the renowned John Angell James had fallen into the snare of seeking popularity some years before, adopting an affected style of preaching. John Elias made this comment on one of his sermons, 'I believe the cross was there, but it was so heaped up with flowers I could not see it.'

As Nonconformists became accepted by society, so society was accepted by Nonconformity. The idea that the successful church is the socially busy church began to be popular and sermons on moral, literary and social topics became more frequent towards the end of the century. The churches became an accepted local 'institution'. When the universities were opened to non-Anglicans in 1871, the old tradition of the Dissenting Academy (colleges for Nonconformists) which taught all subjects died out. Now they taught only theology, but in a newly 'academic' manner, there being a strong desire on the part of Nonconformist scholars to be equal to the universities. This was just the kind of soil needed for theological liberalism to flourish. The colleges were responsible, more than any other section, for the introduction of destructive critical theology into this country and into the churches.

These changes had begun to take place in English Nonconformity well before Poole-Connor was born, but they had little effect on individual congregations until some while after the 1859 Revival. Even when congregations began to seek social respectability, the Spirit of God did not forsake them immediately, as if God were giving them time to recover themselves. Trinity Chapel, Hackney, was an example of a church that remained outside the main current, and retained its orthodoxy. In general, however, very few people recognised the gradual decline in spirituality and doctrinal faithfulness that was taking place. On the surface, everything seemed to be progressing well. Numbers continued to increase long after the old fervour began to run down. Eventually, in the 20th century, the increasingly superficial state of Nonconformity would be laid bare, and the true cause of its condition seen.

The mid-19th century had been the climax of a 'golden age' in many ways. It was certainly rich in the spiritual privileges that God granted to English Nonconformity, and which had been handed down from previous generations. However, there were few that appreciated them sufficiently to pass them on to their succeeding generation. Poole-Connor was one of the few.

Notes

1   *Evangelical Magazine & Missionary Chronicle*, Williams & Son, London, 1851.
2   R. Tudur Jones, *Congregationalism in England 1662-1962*, Independent Press, London, 1962, p. 248.
3   J. Waddington, *Congregational History*, pp. 147-148.
4   Tudur Jones, ibid., p. 253.
5   W. Hale White, *The Early Life of Mark Rutherford*, Oxford University Press, 1913, p. 16.
6   J. W. Grant, *Free Churchmanship in England*, 1870-1940, Independent Press, London, 1958, pp. 5-6.
7   J. R. Thompson, *The Idea of the Church Regarded in its Historical Development*, p. 125.
8   Grant, ibid., p. 18.
9   A. W. W. Dale, *The Life of R. W. Dale of Birmingham*, Hodder & Stoughton, 1898, p. 391.
10 G. M. Trevelyan, *English Social History*, The Reprint Society, 1948, p. 533.
11 Trevelyan, ibid., p. 514.
12 K. Feiling, *History of England*, Macmillan, 1951, p. 897.
13 E. Routley, *English Religious Dissent*, Cambridge University Press, 1960.

4

An Example of Unsound Influence

WE SHALL now look at the vital period which marks the turning point in the life of the churches of God in the United Kingdom – events that took place before Poole-Connor's twenty-first birthday in 1893. Since he covered this period in great detail in his own writings, we not only have the opportunity of quoting extensive passages from him, but also of seeing what lay behind his watchfulness in later developments. He was anxious to provide true unity by bringing the sheep together, but also to drive out the wolves. The period we are to review reveals just how tightly the wolf holds on to the fleece.

We have seen that during the reign of Queen Victoria the influence of biblical Christianity reached every part of the country, so much so that the strength of evangelicalism in the 19th century cannot be ignored by the secular historian. D. C. Somervell has pointed out that evangelicalism was the chief ingredient of that state of mind called Victorianism; and R. C. K. Ensor tells us, 'No one will ever understand Victorian England who does not appreciate that among highly civilised . . . countries, it was one of the most religious that the world had ever known.'[1]

Yet, for all this, when the 19th century closed, the drift from vital godliness was so marked that Somervell said of 20th-century England, 'Never, perhaps, before has so large a part of the population abandoned all interest in what the wisest of all ages have regarded as the fundamental problems of life, the problems of religion.'[2]

Chapter 9 of Poole-Connor's book, *Evangelicalism in England*, is entitled 'The Nineteenth Century: Flood-tide and Ebb'. The question naturally arises, how could there be *such* an ebb after *such* a flood-tide? What was the cause of the 'ebb' of Christianity that followed so rapidly after such great success? The usual answer given is the arrival of the theory of evolution and the higher criticism that accompanied it. However, it is no more accurate to wholly blame the great change on these than to blame Samson's capture on the Philistines. Just as Samson foolishly put *himself* into the hands of those who ruined him, so evangelical leaders consorted with false teachers who took away their faithfulness and power. The people of God themselves were responsible for the great apostasy.

When Poole-Connor referred to the damaging inertia on the part of evangelicals towards modernism, he held them chiefly responsible for the fact that 'the ebb-tide now runs like a mill-race'. A careful study of the way in which higher criticism entered into the life of Nonconformity, and took almost complete control, reveals the truth of this statement.

The face of England was rapidly changing during the Industrial Revolution. The idea of 'progress' was gathering momentum. The size of Nonconformity was growing enormously, although while the Gospel spread its influence, at the same time it became an increasingly shallow Gospel. Larger numbers were affected than ever before, but real spiritual power decreased. As the Nonconformists, who had been denied many rights in the world, were emancipated, so they sought to use their influence in the world outside; but while they succeeded in infiltrating into every part (even to the point where the Prime Minister, Lloyd-George, was Chairman of the Free Church Council), the world infiltrated into the churches. Evangelicals began to work together as never before, yet by the end of the 19th century modernism had gained almost complete control in the running of the main denominations.

An outstanding event that followed the 1859 Revival was the phenomenon of D. L. Moody's missions. Some space will be devoted to Moody's missions, since they played an important part in influencing the life of evangelicalism in England. D. L. Moody first came to England in 1873, Poole-Connor telling the story in *Evangelical Unity*:

'He had been invited to undertake a mission . . . with a promise of funds to meet the travelling expenses of his party. But no funds came: and when, after finding the passage money himself, he landed in Liverpool, it was to learn that his three friends and guarantors had passed away. An unopened letter in his pocket led him to York, where mission services were arranged. The beginnings were quite small.'

From here Moody went on to Sunderland, being received with some reserve at first, but increasingly winning his way. From Sunderland he went on to Newcastle-upon-Tyne, where many people of the educated class were among the converts; and shortly after to Edinburgh. The experiences there exceeded all expectations. Wherever Moody preached, the churches were filled to overflowing, with hundreds turned away. This could be explained by the fact that so many churches joined together to support him.

'Moody's visit to Glasgow was attended with equal or even greater results. The final meeting was of a most impressive character. It was held in the Botanical Gardens on a Sunday evening. *[Moody's son wrote]* "Mr Sankey *[Moody's worship leader and singer]* found his way into the building and began the service with six or seven thousand people who were crushed together there: but so great was the crowd outside, estimated at twenty to thirty thousand, that Mr Moody himself could not get inside. Standing on the coachman's box of the carriage in which he was driven, he asked the members of the choir to sing . . . and then preached for an hour on 'Immediate Salvation'. So distinct was his voice that the great crowd could hear him without difficulty."'

After visiting various parts of Scotland and Ireland, Moody went on to the larger cities and towns of England. Poole-Connor later regarded the campaign as not only a great evangelistic mission, but a powerful influence in the movement towards the togetherness of evangelicals. 'This movement of the Spirit of God was a homily on the subject of Christian unity.'

However, there was another feature of the Moody missions that must be related in order to complete the picture, for theological liberalism in the form of higher criticism was seeping into the life of the churches even at the level of missions. Henry Drummond was at the very centre of the Moody campaigns, but soon embraced the 'new thought', and finally adopted beliefs that invalidated the Gospel itself. His biographer, George Adam Smith, tells us that his career 'is typical of the influence upon the older Christian orthodoxy of the three great intellectual movements of our time – historical criticism, physical science, and socialism'.[3] What happened to Drummond subsequently happened to thousands, many through his example. Owing to the prominent position he was given by Moody, he wielded a vast influence over people, and this clearly led many to adopt the devastating principles of higher criticism.

Henry Drummond came from a godly home, and was 'trained in an evangelical family, and in the school of the older orthodoxy'.

He did not seem to have any spiritual struggles as a youth. 'To Drummond the Christian experience of faith was not so much of struggle as of growth.'[4] His godly upbringing preserved him, to start with, from error. At the Free Church College he retained orthodox convictions, holding to an evangelical view of the inspiration of Scripture, but only until he returned to college after the Moody missions. He was a charming person, and a perfect gentleman, with a genius for friendship. It was recorded that he appeared to have few cares in life, no sorrows, and was seldom overworked.

He came into contact with Moody during the mission to Edinburgh, the feature that chiefly attracted him being the 'novel enquiry meetings'. To Drummond's own mind, this aspect of the mission must have appeared its most surprising element. Here was the very factor which he had missed in the church to which he belonged, and for which he had been pleading (especially in an essay to the Theological Society[5]). He had contrasted the clinical work of a medical student with the total absence of any direct dealing with people in the church's teaching ministry, and had maintained that a minister can do far more good by 'buttonholing' individuals than by preaching sermons. The essay was understood to be purely speculative. But within a month D. L. Moody had arrived, and Drummond was able to put his speculations into practice in the enquiry meetings.[6]

He was struck by Moody's sincerity 'and the practical wisdom of the new methods'. For his part, Moody was feeling the need of a young man to take charge of the meetings for young men. At first Drummond, like other students, was employed only in the enquiry room. 'Often he was to be seen going home through the streets after a meeting with a man in whose arm his own was linked.' Moody soon made it his policy to appoint Drummond to continue the work among the young men at places which Sankey and he had visited. His biographer says: 'He had a great power over individuals. He would keep up a constant confessional, the success of the work obviously dependent upon his presence, ministers and leading lay-men in many towns looking to him as their chief, the sense (right or wrong) that the Christianity of the next generation in these places might largely be determined by the work he had charge of.'[7]

Indeed, the Christianity of the next generation *was* influenced by him, but what kind of Christianity was it? He was only twenty-three when he was brought right into the centre of the mission work, and he was enthusiastic for it. 'I do not believe there has ever been such an opportunity for work in the history of the church,' he said in 1874, when in Londonderry with Moody. 'Moody says, if the young men's meetings can be kept up in every town, he believes there will be 10,000 young men converted before the winter is over.'

Though George Adam Smith speaks highly of the missions as a whole, he points out that large numbers of converts fell away. Num-bers were frequently exaggerated, and time was not given for people to consider the message before they were urged to respond. Balleine makes this comment about the Moody missions: 'In the midst of the great evangelistic campaign, a feeling of dissatisfaction had begun to make itself felt.'[8] This was Drummond's own experience, and he decided to return to the Free Church College. He was influenced in his decision by the mother of a friend of his, with whom he had a long talk, and who showed him (to use his own words), 'how the evangelist's career was apt to be a failure – perhaps a few years of enthusiasm and blessing, then carelessness: no study, no spiritual fruits; too often a sad collapse'.[9]

Moody was most anxious for him to go across to the United States to help him. 'My dear Drummond, I am glad I went to England to learn how to reach young men. Could you come over and help us? I think you would get a few thousand souls on these shores, if you should come. Come if you possibly can . . .'[10] Clearly, Drummond was valued most because of the influence he had over people. George Adam Smith several times compares him to a medieval saint: 'One man said to me only the other day, "Since Drummond died I have not been able to help praying to him."' R. R. Simpson contributed the following remark: 'At an enquiry meeting in the Assembly Hall I spoke to a bright-looking young man, and found that he had decided for Christ. On my asking him what led him to a decision, the striking answer was, "It was the way Mr Drummond laid his hand on my shoulder and looked me in the face that led me to Christ."'[11]

In a lecture on 'The New Evangelism', delivered to the Free Church Theological Society shortly before his death, Drummond describes the alarmingly shallow conception he had of evangelism while he was at college, and during the Moody missions: 'I do not acquit myself of blame here, and I hope no one else has an experience so shocking, but until well on in my college course, and after hearing hundreds of sermons and addresses on the person and work of Christ, the ruling idea left in my mind was that Christ was a mere convenience. The prime end of religion was to get off, the plan of salvation was an elaborate scheme for getting off; and after a man had faced the scheme, understood it, agreed to it, the one thing needful was secured.'[12]

This is surely a solemn insight into the kind of advice Drummond gave to enquirers. Yet even at the end of his life, Moody thought very highly of him. 'Never have I known a man,' wrote Moody in 1897, 'who, in my opinion, lived nearer the Master, or sought to do His will more fully.' The feeling was mutual. A month before his death Drummond said to one of his doctors, 'Moody was the biggest human I ever met.'

Should we blame Moody for not detecting Drummond's lack of doctrinal substance? Not altogether, since, in common with others like him, the latter was careful to hide it. When criticised from all quarters he denied that he had changed on fundamental doctrines (even when he received reproof from Sankey). This attitude was dangerous in the extreme. It was what he *did not* say that worried his friends, what he left out.

Drummond's startling position comes out in his lecture on 'The New Evangelism' previously referred to. He admitted that his thought verged on danger, stating in plain terms that theology 'is a thing that moves', and that there is 'a progress in truth itself'. He said: 'The Bible is not a system . . . its truth is without form . . . and it is in this elasticity that one finds a sanction for a new theology to be the basis of a new evangelism.' Drummond rejected much of the Old Testament, saying, 'The Old Testament believer, I need not remind you, was very helpless as to a personal God. Each man, practically, had to make an image of God for himself.' He also said, 'The emphasis on the humanity of Christ *[preaching Christ as an example of a great human being rather than as divine]* which, happily, has now crept into our best teaching, marks more distinctly perhaps than anything else the dawn of the new evangelism.'

If he had published such views a few years before, there would have been an uproar. However, he was careful even then to present his views to those who were the least likely to disagree with them, and who were themselves careful not to let people know what they really believed.

How did Moody make the mistake of giving such a man the opportunity to influence so many to such a serious degree? It was a simple one. He mistook nature for grace. It is perfectly clear that Drummond was one of the most gracious people you could wish to meet. His godly upbringing gave him sound views, but as he grew older, since they were not really his own, they gradually disappeared. He was attracted to Moody as a *person* – the greatest 'human' he had ever met. He emphasised the 'humanity' of Christ, and proclaimed His love as a love which was essentially human rather than divine. Drummond stands out as both a representative and a leader of those who had all the privileges of the rich

Nonconformist heritage of the mid-19th century, and exchanged it for a Christianity which was gradually being de-spiritualised.

Poole-Connor, on the other hand, was both a representative and a leader of those who appreciated that heritage, and, together with a godly remnant, defended it. He likewise was a perfect gentleman, but this did not prevent him from being a 'Valiant for Truth'.

Doubtless many people were blessed by the Moody missions, and this is widely known and documented, but the historian's task is to present both sides of the picture, however disturbing. Drummond's influence on the ongoing evangelistic missions of D. L. Moody is just one example – and a highly infectious one – of how theological liberalism increasingly penetrated evangelical church life. A new organisation, The Bible League, was commenced in 1892 to counteract the drift. Later, Poole-Connor was to become Editor of its *Quarterly*, and devote much of his life to carefully directing a journal that warned the unwary, and gave scholarly support to the doctrine of verbal inspiration – that every word of the Bible is given by inspiration of God. Poole-Connor was supremely equipped to defend the *old* Gospel and the *old* evangelicalism. He was prepared, furthermore, to look very closely at men like Drummond, and to expose their dangerous teaching.

Lest it should be thought that Poole-Connor was preoccupied with negative critiques, it should be said that his support and endorsement of sound preachers and causes was frequently voiced. He was impressed by many effective ministers during his long life, and delighted to describe his contact with them. He had a gift for describing a person's character and appearance, as can be seen particularly in his *Evangelicalism in England*. There were none, however, who ranked so high in his estimation as C. H. Spurgeon. What impressed him most of all was not his amazing talent, but his utter faithfulness, particularly a willingness to suffer at the hands even of his friends, for the sake of the Gospel. It was true that he excelled his contemporaries in his abilities, in an age of great preachers, but his faithfulness was especially treasured.

On one occasion, when Poole-Connor was ten years old, he was taken to worship at the Metropolitan Tabernacle. As he stood near one of the exits, Mr Spurgeon was escorted out to his carriage. The great man saw him, stopped, shook his hand, and with a kind word left a lasting impression of extreme kindliness and of a face aglow with the love of God. Poole-Connor read much of Spurgeon, shared his theological outlook, and followed him in his steadfastness in the faith. It is no accident that he desired his earthly remains to be buried not many yards from those of Spurgeon.

The Down-Grade Controversy was the most important event for evangelicals in England in the latter part of the 19th century, since, in Poole-Connor's view, 'it came nearer to causing a fundamentalist-modernist split such as later developed in the United States than any other incident among Nonconformists in England.'

In order to understand the Down-Grade, we must consider the forces that had been secretly operating for some time, becoming increasingly active in the 1880s and 1890s. There is a remarkable parallel between the manner in which higher criticism captured the denominations then, and the way in which ecumenism captured them later. As Spurgeon was a watchman in his day, so Poole-Connor later warned of the World Council of Churches and its ultimate purpose. Poole-Connor himself devoted more of his time to defending the doctrine of verbal inspiration than to defending any other doctrine. As one follows events one grows in appreciation of the great stand he took, and the way he conducted himself. He saw that the effect of modernism was to rob people of the Bible, and he constantly exposed it. He defended the inerrant Bible, but what was more important, he saw that the reason why such damaging teaching had so great an influence was because of the passivity and compromise of sound people. Hence, as Paul withstood Peter to the face for the sake of the Gospel, so Poole-Connor frequently had to expose compromise within the ranks of evangelicals. He saw, moreover, that heresy creeps in among God's people in a subtle way. The picture of the infiltration of modernism in the late 19th century is a terrible spectacle of how, through the weakness of good men, unsound, scheming men can gain admission and change the entire position of churches. Poole-Connor, during the latter part of his life, was continually exposing the subtle inroads of modernism.

Notes

1 R. C. K. Ensor, *England 1870-1914*, Clarenden Press, Oxford, 1936.
2 D. C. Somervell, *English Thought in the Nineteenth Century*, David Mckay and Co. Inc., New York, 1940, pp. 234-235.
3 George Adam Smith, *The Life of Henry Drummond*, Hodder & Stoughton, London, 1899, p. 14.
4 Smith, ibid., p. 14.
5 Smith, ibid., p. 46.
6 Smith, ibid., p. 63.
7 Smith, ibid., p. 71.
8 G. R. Balleine, *History of the Evangelical Party in the Church of England*, Longman, Green & Co., London, 1933, p. 232.
9 Smith, ibid., p. 102.
10 Smith, ibid., p. 104.
11 Smith, ibid., p. 98.
12 H. Drummond, *The New Evangelism and Other Papers*, Hodder & Stoughton, London, 1899, p. 15.

5

Heritage Lost
How Higher Criticism Gained a Foothold

T HE THEORY of biological evolution raised doubts regarding the uniqueness of man and the factor of original sin; but the greatest difficulty was its contradiction of *Genesis*. The Bible had gained a foremost place in the life of the nation since the Reformation, and especially in the Puritan era, when – 'England became the people of a book, and that book was the Bible.'[1] Since then it had entered into every strand of religious and secular life and thought. The Protestant principle that every man should read the Bible for himself, had given it a central place in family life and in the religious experience of the individual. The 18th-century evangelical revival had put such an emphasis on the Bible, that it held a place in England scarcely equalled in the rest of Christendom. Bound up, inevitably, with faith in the Book, was the belief in that Book's divine inspiration and infallibility. However, it had never been attacked in the way that it was now to be assaulted.

The comparative ease with which higher criticism gained entrance into English churches in the latter part of the 19th century was due to the fact that it became acceptable to many who were within the churches. Remarkably, the authority of the Bible had never before been seriously questioned by people *within* the professing church. Attacks launched by the 18th-century deists,* for example, had been from outside, and had been aimed at the Christian faith as a whole. Then it was essential to defend the Bible in order to defend the Christian faith. When, however, the Bible was attacked from *within,* by those who imagined that the evangelical faith could survive without an inerrant Bible, higher criticism seemed interesting and acceptable.

The home of higher criticism was the German universities, where theological professors were paid by the State. They claimed to be seeking to understand the Bible, not to destroy it. However, they explained the religious development of the Old Testament in terms of evolution, whereas traditional evangelicals attributed it to the unfolding revelation of God. The reaction to this form of unbelief coming from Germany was the formation of an opposing school of thought in this country, the most prominent members being scholars such as Westcott, Lightfoot and Hort, of Cambridge. But these were themselves higher critics, and did not disagree with the idea of approaching the Bible with a critical attitude. They simply reacted against the extremes of German higher criticism which came from theologians who had little time for the Christian faith. These scholarly defenders of the Bible would soon come out in their true colours, undermining evangelicalism.

Higher criticism did not get a foothold in England until after 1880, but before then the way was being prepared by men who appeared to be entirely orthodox. In 1860 the controversy began,

---

*Those who believed in a kind of God, but not in the revelation of the Bible.

but even in 1880 it could be claimed that ninety-nine percent of the biblical scholars of England, Scotland and America believed that Moses was the author of the first five books of the Bible, as the Bible says. Ten years later, however, the percentage was very different, the percentage rejecting Mosaic authorship having risen sharply.

As soon as higher criticism was introduced into this country by somewhat more orthodox clergy and ministers, it began to be examined sympathetically. As long as the higher criticism had seemed to be in the hands of extremists, there had been little fear of it.

The very first controversy over higher criticism in Britain centred on a Congregationalist named Samuel Darwin, who, in 1856, published alarming views on inspiration. He had little influence, however, because he made the fatal mistake of combining his higher criticism with a tendency towards liberal theology.[2] The liberal scholar Albert Schweitzer has an interesting comment in this context: 'The fact is that in theology the most revolutionary ideas are swallowed quite readily so long as they smooth their passage by a few small concessions. It is only when a spicule of bone stands out obstinately and causes choking that theology begins to take note of dangerous ideas.'[3]

An example of the unwillingness of evangelicals to accept higher criticism from extremists was the reaction to Bishop Colenso's *The Pentateuch and Book of Joshua Critically Examined*, in which he denounced as untrustworthy large sections, even whole books, of the Old Testament, declaring them to be deliberate fabrications designed to deceive. This was too much, too suddenly. W. B. Glover comments, 'one cannot but admire his honesty . . . but he was singularly lacking in political sense.' Perhaps it was 'political sense' that moved T. K. Cheyne, a significant Anglican scholar, to take up a somewhat 'evangelical' position. Early in his career he had attacked the evangelical defence of the Bible, but at that time he was too close to German rationalists to have much influence. It was only after his apparent move towards evangelicalism that his influence became widespread.

A. B. Davidson, a professor in New College, Edinburgh, began in the early 1870s to introduce many of the ablest students of the Free Church to the higher criticism of the Pentateuch. His evangelical position was so respected that he was actually given scope to defend higher criticism in the pages of the *British and Foreign Evangelical Review*. His remarks, however, were in general terms, and aroused no suspicions about his general orthodoxy. Glover tells us, 'Davidson was extremely wary of committing himself in print on specific points of criticism.' It is owing to his great caution that he succeeded in laying a foundation for higher criticism in Scotland.

English Nonconformists leaned heavily on the work of the Cambridge trio – Westcott, Lightfoot and Hort – for their defence of the New Testament against higher criticism, but as a result they accepted the germs of higher criticism that were embedded in that defence. Higher criticism was being accepted in principle, while the conclusions of the extreme modernists were rejected.

With the project to produce *The Revised Version* of the Bible in 1881, the issue of higher criticism was brought to the fore. Many evangelicals were looking for some explanation or theory of inspiration that would allow for the possibility of errors in the Bible, yet at the same time guarantee its objective authority as a final court of appeal in doctrinal matters. It was a false hope, embodying a fundamental contradiction, but it had immense influence in the development of religious opinion in England. Glover's comments on the condition of things in 1881 are: 'If a vote had been taken, it is certain that the conservative defence of inerrancy made by the Wesleyan *London Quarterly Review* would have been found to represent the majority of Nonconformists, rather than the looser view of the *British Quarterly Review*. But too many people of unquestioned evangelical faith had renounced inerrancy for any strong defence against higher criticism to be made at this point.'[4]

Thus the doors to higher criticism had been opened by men of 'unquestioned evangelical faith'. The pew did not want it, but the men in the pulpit wanted above all to be 'in the fashion'.

There came about (in Glover's words) a 'general lack of interest among evangelicals in theology. The pietistic quality of the revival starting in 1859 put primary emphasis on individual Christian experience, and tended to value sound doctrine only as a means to that end. As a result, evangelicals would tolerate almost any divergence in doctrine provided the individual concerned was known to have a fervent evangelical experience, and above all, if his ministry awakened the same experience in others.'[5]

The low state of discernment about higher criticism is seen in the annual address to the Evangelical Alliance in 1869, delivered by the Principal of the Wesleyan Training Institute, Westminster, an ardent evangelical. In an optimistic report on the state of evangelicalism throughout the world, he paid his respects to the great Bible scholars of Germany and France: 'We may not accept all their expositions, but unquestionably they hold the root faith in divine revelation and in the person of the Lord Jesus Christ, and the tenor of their lives is holy.'[6] Such praise, coming from such a quarter, was bound to make it easy for higher criticism to gain an entrance with the unwary.

Increasingly, in the resolving of apparent problems in the Bible, reliance was placed on the outcome of scholarly research, and the acceptance of higher criticism in principle followed. Main-line evangelicals were thus led to approach the Bible in the same way as the higher critics. Though they knew it was a revelation from God, they approached it as though they were in a position to make an independent enquiry into its contents. With many of the Nonconformist leaders, as soon as higher criticism was presented to them in a way that appeared not to involve a repudiation of their evangelical faith, they were prepared to accept it. W. E. H. Lecky famously pointed out that, 'the success of any opinion *[depends]* much less upon the force of its arguments than upon the predisposition of society to receive it.' They were predisposed by 1880.

Then, between 1880 and 1890 higher criticism came in like a flood. We have already mentioned T. K. Cheyne, the scholar who moved to a largely evangelical position while still embracing higher criticism. He had no great influence until he modified his extreme position, and then his influence became considerable. This is not to charge him with insincerity, but to show how willing evangelicals were to accept the findings of higher criticism if they were presented by a man who appeared to affirm orthodox views.

The *London Quarterly Review*, while still arguing for verbal inspiration, could yet give a very favourable review of Cheyne's exposition of *Jeremiah* in *The Pulpit Commentary*. The reviewer gave an extraordinary assessment of this exposition, calling it – 'complete and exact, taking account of the latest Continental results; orthodox in the best sense, and withal manifesting a reasonable and intelligent sympathy with the honest inquiries of the semi-destructive school.'

Evangelicals went through a transitional stage in which they accepted some of the findings of higher criticism and not others. Alexander Maclaren, the great expository preacher of Manchester, is a typical example. He had great influence among the Baptists. He was an important 'mediator' between higher criticism and evangelicals, as William R. Nicoll points out: 'His greatness as a preacher rested upon his emphasis on evangelical certainties rather than on the reconciling of old theology with new theories.'[7] And Glover concurs: 'The example of so great a preacher who was toler-ant of higher criticism, and who even entertained the possibility that the story of the Fall was mythical, could not have been without effect.'[8] His position was so respected, and his life and ministry so exemplary, that though his views must have been known, Spurgeon did not implicate him as one of the Down-Grade preachers. Yet he was undoubtedly in the critical school. He was versed in the work of the critics, and he stood ready to accept whatever they could clearly demonstrate. He managed at the same time to go on using the Bible as a source of infallible texts, even though he did not reject the criticism that had undermined the foundation for such an approach.

Another sad example of a man with a reputation for being orthodox who was yielding to modernism, but who did not let this be known until modernism was widely accepted, is that of R. W. Dale. A majority of evangelicals, it seems, in the 1880s, still accepted the idea of verbal inspiration and the inerrancy of the Bible. To the end of the century the Sunday School teachers were still teaching the Bible as infallible.

Nonconformist leaders occupied the position of 'mediators' between the higher critics and the mass of believing Christians. A. M. Fairbairn, Principal of Mansfield College, Oxford, considered the greatest scholar among Nonconformists, did this task effectively by using the old phraseology while assigning to it a completely different meaning. In this way he kept the confidence of his contemporaries. As Glover constantly affirms, 'In general, higher criticism never caused any alarm as long as it was expressed incidentally to a positive affirmation of evangelical truth.' Ministers were concerned not to disturb their people with higher criticism, yet wanted to introduce it gently. They tended to keep the 'old' interpretations so far as they were not directly contradicted by the higher criticism they accepted. Some accepted more than others, and each found his own compromise, but the compromises effected by individuals between 'tradition' and 'criticism' are well depicted in a figure borrowed from Schweitzer: 'The two are shaken together like water and oil, in which case the semblance of combination is only maintained so long as the shaking continues.'

Spurgeon, however, could see where all this was going to lead, and

that there was no half-way position. He was the first, and one of the
very few, to sound an alarm. But so subtle was the behaviour of the
modernists that even Spurgeon had underestimated the apostasy,
and had sounded the alarm too late. An example of this is seen in
the case of the change of Editor of the *Expositor*, which Spurgeon
welcomed, in 1881. Samuel Cox, the Editor, had adopted the heresy
of universalism, and used the magazine to spread this view further.
W. R. Nicoll was appointed in his place, and this pleased Spurgeon,
but Nicoll did far more to destroy the doctrine of the inspiration of
Scripture than Cox had ever done. Glover gives us the reason: 'The
basic reason is more probably connected with subtle matters of
approach which are almost indefinable.' Nicoll stated a policy that
Nonconformists had long been following when he wrote in 1897,
'The new truths should dawn on the church as gently as the sun-
light, and I am not at all sure but that heretics ought to be burnt. I
mean the fellows who make a big row and split their churches.'[9]

The policy of J. D. Jones provides a good illustration. Succeeding
an older preacher who had held out steadfastly against the critics, he
faced a real problem. Having always spoken freely about the new
liberal ideas of the Bible, he wondered how he would get along with
his new charge. Evidently he did well, for he stayed for thirty-nine
years and claimed he never experienced a church quarrel. His
biographer explains: 'J. D. Jones adapted himself to this change in
mental environment not by altering his own views, but by adjusting
his emphases to the susceptibilities of his new church and congregation. To borrow a phrase used in another connection, he was "wisely
indefinite while ardently believing".'[10]

'There must have been numbers of Nonconformist ministers who
were "secret believers" in higher criticism before 1890. After that
date the tide was running heavily in favour of criticism, and they
could declare their opinions with much greater safety to themselves
and to the religious life of their congregations. Open avowals in the

late eighties and early nineties on the part of men who had been privately convinced before, may help to account for the rapidity with which higher criticism spread after 1887.'[11]

Yet higher criticism had scarcely penetrated beyond the classroom and the study. In June, 1887, Nicoll wrote, 'As yet, comparatively few people understand what the critical position is, and it will never be possible to make it easily intelligible to the multitude. In this way an inevitable conflict may be long postponed.'[12] The battle came with Spurgeon's Down-Grade Controversy in 1887. It was an attempt to draw out the enemy in open battle, but they would not fight. They had succeeded too well by other means.

Glover comments: 'Before 1887, higher criticism had made surprising progress among the most influential Nonconformist leaders, but, partly as a result of their tact and caution, the masses of believers had scarcely realised what was afoot . . . There was no permanent split over higher criticism, due partly to the policy of the leaders and also the absence of a strong evangelical scholarship such as the Princeton School in the USA. The nearest approach to a fundamentalist-modernist split such as came later in the USA was the Down-Grade Controversy . . .

'Spurgeon seems never to have been seriously disturbed in his own personal religious life by anything the critics said . . . The Bible was not for Spurgeon a thing for rational justification; it was the starting point for all right reason on religious matters. He was one of the few men of his generation who really felt more certain of the truth of the Bible than he did of the truth of contemporary science. If geology was in conflict with the Bible, then so much the worse for geology.'[13]

The Down-Grade was for Poole-Connor the most important event that happened during his lifetime. Indeed, he referred to it more frequently than to anything else that has taken place in this country. He considered that it was of the utmost importance that evangelicals should acquaint themselves with the facts. He described the Down-Grade in great detail in *Evangelicalism in England*, and in a chapter in *The Apostasy of English Nonconformity*. He issued a booklet at the centenary of Spurgeon's birth (which will be quoted in a later chapter). It is for this reason we must treat this subject at length, describing the details of the controversy. We are able to quote largely from Poole-Connor's *The Apostasy of English Non-conformity*, which is not only out of print but almost unobtainable.

In March and April of 1887, two articles entitled 'The Down-Grade' appeared in *The Sword and the Trowel*. These were not by Spurgeon, and sketched instances of how error had infiltrated the ranks of evangelicals in the past. The writer warned of the danger of departing from the inspiration of Scripture, which was the only foundation of faith. No serious concern was aroused until Spurgeon himself contributed a third article (in August, 1887) in which he described the current decline of sound doctrine among Dissenters, and gave illustrations without mentioning names. His attack was on theological heresy, and he opposed higher criticism because it led to apostasy from the Truth. In other words, he associated higher criticism with the denial of sound doctrine. It was because of his grasp of systematic theology that he saw in higher criticism an essential conflict with evangelical truth. To him there was no half-way position.

Glover declared: 'What Spurgeon was opposing was a theological trend, a tendency towards a relaxation of older views, a confusion and uncertainty that bred a tolerance of nearly all opinions provided they were held by men who also declared themselves evangelical. As to the facts, Spurgeon was clearly in the right.'[14] His insight into the religious life of his own times was proved by the events that followed.

Spurgeon charged his contemporaries with denying the inspiration of the Scriptures. For their part, these claimed that they still believed this, and were theologically sound. In reality they were utterly compromised, but accused Spurgeon of being vague in his charges. We now quote Poole-Connor's description of Down-Grade events:

'The article in which he [Spurgeon] first sounded the alarm was written in 1887, and appeared in *The Sword and the Trowel* for August. The tone of it may be judged from the following extract: "Read those newspapers which represent the broad school of Dissent, and ask yourself – How much further will they go? . . . The atonement is scouted, the inspiration of Scripture derided, the punishment of sin is turned into a fiction, and the resurrection into a myth . . . It now becomes a serious question how far those who abide by the Truth once delivered unto the saints should fraternise with those who have turned aside to another Gospel."

'This article, and those which followed, aroused the strongest possible feeling, both of assent and dissent. While many confirmed the necessity for Mr Spurgeon's protest, others charged him with gross exaggeration, or with sowing discord amongst brethren. Some resorted to personalities, and, affecting to attribute his article to the depression of ill-health, advised him to take a long rest. Others, again, found in the subject a source of merriment. A month later Mr Spurgeon returned to the charge: "We have received abundant proofs," he wrote, "that our alarm was none too soon. Letters from all quarters declare that the case of the church at this present is worse than we thought it to be . . . A chasm is opening . . . Let us take our places, not in anger, nor in the spirit of suspicion or division, but in watchfulness and resolve."

'To those who charged Spurgeon with "sour pessimism", he replied: "We are denounced as gloomy. Well, well! The day was when we were censured for being wickedly humorous, and many were the floggings we received for our unseemly jests. So the world's opinion changes. A half-a-farthing would be an extravagant price to pay for its verdict one way or another . . ."'

Spurgeon was not bitter towards his opponents. W. Fuller Gooch, pastor at West Norwood, declared, 'I have myself again and again knelt by his side when he has poured out his heart in loving prayer for those from whom he had to differ so openly and so firmly.'

Spurgeon's ministerial followers were only a minority. Even respected evangelicals declared their faith in the soundness of the evangelical ministry. The president of the London Baptist Association confused the issue by saying, 'There never was a period in English history when there was so much earnest evangelical work done, and done mainly through our churches, as today.'

Spurgeon was puzzled and exasperated, and in the October 1887 issue of *The Sword and the Trowel* he published his third article, 'The Case Proved', writing: 'Our warning was intended to call attention to an evil which we thought was apparent to all: we never dreamed ... that a company of esteemed friends would rush in between the combatants, and declare that there was no cause for war ... Yet such has been the case, and in many quarters the main question has been not "How can we remove the evil?" but "Is there any evil to remove?" No end of letters have been written with this as their theme – "Are the charges made by Mr Spurgeon at all true?"'

In the article that followed Spurgeon showed the truth of his allegations, but refrained from naming any particular people. He had ample evidence. *The Christian World*, one of Spurgeon's most outspoken antagonists, far from denying the prevalence of 'modern thought', gloried in it, and taunted those who endeavoured to conceal the facts. Spurgeon pointed out the denominational loyalty that had contributed to those opposed to his warning. 'Brethren who have been officials of a denomination have a paternal partiality about them which is so natural, and so sacred, that we have not the heart to censure it. Above all things, these prudent brethren feel bound to preserve the prestige of "the body", and the peace of the committee. Our Unions, Boards, and Associations are so justly dear to the fathers, that quite unconsciously and innocently, they grow oblivious of evils which, to the unofficial mind, are as manifest as the sun in the heavens. This could not induce our honoured brethren to be untruthful; but it does influence them in their judgement and still more in the expression of that judgement.'

He was doubtless surprised at the unexpected opposition he met. In November[*] he resigned from the Baptist Union. He called attention to the 'wretched spectacle' of orthodox Christians in avowed religious union with those who had denied the faith. 'To be very plain, we are unable to call these things Christian Unions, they begin to look more like Confederacies in Evil.'

Poole-Connor continues, 'At the close of his article Mr Spurgeon indicated what he felt must be his attitude to the Baptist Union, which included some who no longer held the orthodox position. "We cannot," he said, "be expected to meet in any union which comprehends those whose teaching is on fundamental matters exactly the reverse of that which we hold dear . . . Garibaldi complained that by the cession of Nice to France he had been made a foreigner in his native land: our heart is burdened with a similar sorrow." "We retire at once," he wrote later, "from the Baptist Union . . . It has no disciplinary powers, and no doctrinal basis whatsoever, and we see no reason why every form of belief and misbelief should not be comprehended in it . . . Those who originally founded it made it 'without form and void' and so it must remain." '

The Baptist Union Council's answer to Spurgeon's charges was an illustration of the frame of mind of many of the evangelical leaders. Glover comments, 'They took the position that his charges were too vague to merit serious investigation, that he had failed to substantiate them by naming any ministers who were guilty. However useful this policy might have been politically, it can only be described as

---

[*]Spurgeon's letter of withdrawal is dated October 28th, 1887.

dishonest trifling with the subject. Spurgeon's resentment was well founded . . . The dishonesty of the Council's position lay in the fact that the Vice-President and several members were themselves in fundamental disagreement with Spurgeon on the specific issues involved. Clifford and his chief supporters, Alexander Maclaren and Charles Williams, had rejected the doctrine of the inerrancy of the Scriptures and were well aware that one distinguished Baptist minister, Samuel Cox, had made himself one of the best-known exponents of universal restoration. Under these circumstances the demand that Spurgeon substantiate his charges by naming guilty persons could have been only a political manoeuvre.'[15]

At the Baptist Union annual meeting everyone expected a fight, but Dr Clifford cleverly avoided it. He skilfully united the assembly in his opening address in the morning, and that afternoon a declaration of the evangelical principles for which the Union had always stood was passed by two thousand to seven. Only a few ministers followed Spurgeon out of the Union; even his brother James remained.

Poole-Connor continues: 'On this ground Mr Spurgeon felt it useless to bring any cases of heterodoxy before it; but pleaded that the Baptist Union should adopt a credal basis similar to that of the Evangelical Alliance. Not only was this refused, but the Council of the Baptist Union stated that a creed in any form was objectionable, and would come between man and his God: a position which Mr Spurgeon strongly controverted, asserting that "The objection to a creed is a very pleasant way of concealing objection to discipline, and a desire for latitudinarianism. What is wished for is a Union which will, like Noah's Ark, afford shelter both for the clean and the unclean, for creeping things and winged fowls." But the Baptist Union steadily refused to accede to his request, and passed upon him a resolution of censure.'

Poole-Connor, writing in 1933, refers to the suffering Spurgeon underwent: 'It may not be known that the controversy caused Mr Spurgeon himself much suffering. For instance, several wealthy people who had helped to maintain his institutions withdrew their support because of his action. Moreover, the strain of the struggle told seriously upon his health, and, in Mrs Spurgeon's judgement, hastened his end. When he left for Menton, where he died, he said to a friend, "Goodbye, Ellis, this fight is killing me." In the sense, therefore, in which we speak of a man who loses his life through devotion to scientific research being a martyr to science, so we may speak of Mr Spurgeon, who suffered much, and whose life was shortened on account of his devotion to Christian Truth, as a martyr to Truth.'

What must have been most painful of all to Spurgeon was the fact that fellow evangelicals of prominence completely let him down. He had expected some support from them, but was left almost alone. At Spurgeon's funeral there were many ready to praise him who had kept silent in the hour of crisis. 'It was not only the genius that we admired,' said Dr Alexander Maclaren, standing by Spurgeon's bier, 'it was the profound faith, the earnestness, the devotion, the self-oblivion, which endeared him to so many hearts and were the secret of his power.' Yet Dr Maclaren had been a member of the very council that censured Spurgeon, and there is no indication that he raised a protest. Carlile records, 'He counted on far larger support than he received: he was humiliated and could not get away from the idea that he had been betrayed.'[16]

Poole-Connor adds: 'Dr J. C. Carlile once preached a sermon from the text "Thou stoodest on the other side", in the course of which he delivered a powerful reproof to those who in any hour of crisis failed to support a righteous cause. When Mr Spurgeon took his stand for orthodoxy many even of those who had been trained in his college (Dr Carlile being one of them) "stood on the other side". But Mr Spurgeon cleared his conscience; and his is the reward of the watchman, who, apprehending danger, fails not to lift his trumpet in warning.'

Let Spurgeon conclude this chapter with his own estimate of the problem: 'We have nowadays around us a class of men who preach Christ, and even preach the Gospel; but then they preach a great deal else which is not true, and thus destroy the good of all that they deliver, and lure men to error. They would be styled "evangelical" and yet be of the school which is really anti-evangelical. Look well to these gentlemen. I have heard that a fox, when close hunted by dogs, will pretend to be one of them, and run with the pack. That is what certain are aiming at just now: *the foxes would seem to be dogs*. But in the case of the fox, his strong scent betrays him, and the dogs soon find him out; and even so, the scent of false doctrine is not easily concealed, and the game does not answer for long. There are extant ministers of whom we scarce can tell whether they are dogs or foxes; but all men shall know *our* quality as long as we live, and they shall be in no doubt as to what we believe and teach. We shall not hesitate to speak in the strongest Saxon words we can find, and in the plainest sentences we can put together, that which we hold as fundamental Truth.'[17]

The events of this review of the loss of the Nonconformist evangelical heritage largely took place within the first twenty-one years of Poole-Connor's life. He saw their significance even in his early years, and he would look on with dismay as their consequences unfolded before his maturer eyes.

Notes

1   J. R. Green, *Short History of the English People*, Ch. 8, 'Puritan England'.
2   W. B. Glover, *Evangelical Nonconformists and Higher Criticism in the 19th Century*, Independent Press, London, 1954, p. 45.
3   Albert Schweitzer, *The Quest of the Historical Jesus*, (Translator: W. Montgomery), A. & C. Black, London, 1910, p. 37.
4   Glover, ibid., p. 90.
5   Glover, ibid., p. 93.

6 Glover, ibid., pp. 101-102.
7 William R. Nicoll, *Princes of the Church*, 4th ed., Hodder & Stoughton, London, 1921, pp. 250-251.
8 Glover, ibid., p. 139 – see Alexander Maclaren, *Expositions of Holy Scripture, Genesis*, New York, 1904, p. 6.
9 Glover, ibid., p. 152.
10 Glover, ibid., p. 153.
11 Glover, ibid., p. 157.
12 Glover, ibid., p. 158.
13 Glover, ibid., p. 163.
14 Glover, ibid., p. 166.
15 Glover, ibid., pp. 172-173.
16 J. C. Carlile, *C. H. Spurgeon*, p. 245.
17 C. H. Spurgeon, *The Greatest Fight in the World*, p. 39.

6

The Battle Entered
A Young Minister Becomes Aware

A YEAR AFTER Spurgeon died, and shortly after his twenty-first birthday, Poole-Connor was called to the pastorate of Aldershot Baptist Church. Previous to this call, in the spring of 1893, he took a 'holiday' on the North Sea coast helping the Mission to Deep Sea Fishermen, keeping a diary of the trip, illustrated with his own fine paintings of ships, sailors and sea creatures. This diary is significant because it shows that at an early age he commanded a wide vocabulary and impressive flow of language, reflecting a well-instructed mind, trained by his considerable appetite for reading. His ministry at Aldershot made immediate progress, including the building of a new hall for an enlarged Sunday School, drawing congratulatory letters from Mrs C. H. Spurgeon, among others. In a little over a year, he was also appointed Baptist Chaplain to the Aldershot Garrison, the first Baptist Chaplain to be appointed in Britain.

There is a remarkable example of Poole-Connor's unusual ability at twenty-two, in a long article on religious delusion published in a popular Christian magazine. It exhibits a clarity, force, perception, fluency and style rarely seen outside mature penmen.

Poole-Connor received considerable help in his early ministry from Dr John Gritton who had succeeded to the pastorate of Trinity Chapel, Hackney. Ordained a Church of England clergyman, and for a time a missionary in India, he had left the Anglican church in 1890, after an incident which gave great gains to the high-church movement within Anglicanism. This was known as the 'Lincoln Judgement'. The Bishop of Lincoln had been charged (by Anglican evangelicals) with illegal practices in the conduct of divine service, namely, Catholic ritual. When judgement was given in the Bishop's favour, the evangelicals abandoned their policy of prosecuting offenders. Most, however, did not favour secession, but felt that they could exert an influence for good on the church. 'I charge my brethren,' wrote Bishop Ryle, 'not to listen for a moment to those who counsel secession. I have no sympathy with the rash and impatient men who recommend such a step. So long as the Articles and Prayer Book are not altered, we occupy an impregnable position. We have an open Bible, and our pulpits are free.'[1] The great man therefore attempted compromise, but Dr Gritton showed strong conviction, and this was the veteran minister who greatly influenced Poole-Connor.

In 1895, Poole-Connor married Edith Ford, whom he had known since boyhood. They were to have five children, two, sadly, dying in infancy. Then, at twenty-six, Poole-Connor was called to the pastorate of Borough Road Baptist Church, Southwark (near the Elephant and Castle, in London). Here he was brought in touch with the poverty, sin and crime of an inner city area, gaining an intimate acquaintance with the conditions of wretchedness and misery under which teeming thousands of very poor people lived. His adaptability was demonstrated in a flourishing ministry.

At this time, just before the turn of the century, the country was still strongly Protestant, even though true evangelicalism was in decline. Evangelicals in the Church of England were finding the tide increasingly going against them, Prebendary Webb-Peploe,[*] one of their leading figures, making this comment:

'While the middle ranks of the English nation remain essentially Protestant and evangelical . . . the power has unquestionably passed (both in church and State) into the hands of those whose tastes, sympathies, and practices are all against what is called "old-fashioned evangelicalism"; and it is idle to deny that the position of evangelical churchmen is in the present day one of general contempt and neglect from those in authority, though in the heart of the nation, if once roused to give expression to its feelings, there can be little doubt that the verdict would be strongly against any attempt at assimilation or union with Rome, and strongly in favour of simple evangelical teaching and practice.'[2]

In 1900, Poole-Connor accepted a call to the Baptist church at Surbiton, a pastorate he described in his book *Evangelical Unity*. 'During the last years of Queen Victoria's reign, and throughout that of King Edward VII, I was pastor of a small flock in that pleasant suburb, which met for a time in a wooden structure generally known as the Balaclava Baptist Church; and there God was pleased to bless us. Persons from all sections of the Christian church attended the simple services . . . I have always regarded those years as the most fruitful of my life.'

In 1907, the church began to publish a monthly, 48-page magazine, in which we find many instances like the following of his concern for evangelism:

'In addition to our regular work, it is proposed to hold a mission

[*]Prebendary being the title of an honorary Canon – a slightly higher rank of clergy in the Church of England.

in which, if it shall please God, we may hope to begin to reap the harvest of seed sown during the autumn and winter. Concerning this, two things may be said. The first is that we need to put forth every effort to induce those who do not attend any place of worship to come to us – particularly on the last Sunday in each month. Men are not to be hurried into a profession of faith in Christ, and these services will give all who wish the opportunity of hearing the Gospel, and considering their relationship to it. The second thing is that if we desire that the Spirit of God should work in the hearts of men, we must *pray*. Every Monday evening the schoolroom is open from eight till nine for prayer. There are many who would be astonished at the help both they and the church would receive, were they present. It is a serious matter to think how many church members are habitually strangers to the prayer meeting.'

He contributed an account of the work in a volume, *The Baptist Churches of Surrey*, published about 1910, at the end of his pastorate, throwing important light on the pastoral, practical, and energetic spirit of the man who would do so much to shed light on the decline of evangelicalism. 'In 1900 the present pastor was called to the charge. As the work developed, the difficulty of accommodation grew. The one room had to serve for chapel, Sunday School and vestry. For baptisms, we went begging to other churches. Besides which, the walls of the hall moved to and fro before the eyes of friends assembled, when a high wind sprung up; and any portly brother walking rapidly up the aisle caused the whole congregation to swing rhythmically up and down. When one day a visiting minister (arriving somewhat early) opened a door which he thought led into a vestry, but which in reality led into a disused dressing-room for the dancers of a previous period, he not only walked into the room – but walked through the floor.

'And yet that wooden hut was to us what the Tabernacle of the wilderness was to the Jews. It enshrined the glory of God; and there many learnt for the first time the saving power of the living Christ. Dr Barnardo came into the service one Sunday evening not very long before he passed to his rest. The Doctor, as is generally known, was extremely deaf; in consequence of which he could so little enter into the service as to be unable to distinguish the singing, but he wrote the next day, saying: "I could not hear a word the preacher said, but I felt, from that moment I entered, the atmosphere of worship."

'In 1901, special prayer meetings were held that the church might be directed to a site for a permanent building. Very definitely in answer, a plot of land was offered and purchased. Similar meetings were held again, to seek that the financial means might be found with which to build; and in an equally definite manner the way was cleared, and in March 1904, the present church was opened for public worship. Several of the leading men of the Baptist denomination took part. Since then our story has been one of quiet, steady work, and of preaching the Gospel – the old-fashioned Gospel – and we have been increasingly established, we trust, as one of the churches of God planted in the garden of Surrey.'[3]

His ministerial experience at Surbiton was an important factor in the breaking down of his denominationalism. He wrote: 'I became, unwisely, President of the Kingston Free Church Council, and ... was out of my element. I could not, on scriptural grounds, join with other Nonconformists in the Passive Resistance movement. I was expected to exchange pulpits with ministers of modernist views. I found the Baptist Union to be strongly leavened with the same influence. I grew more and more unhappy.'

He reacted away from narrow denominationalism and was drawn into the interdenominational position. He could not feel the same hostility towards evangelical brethren in the Church of England as some of his fellow Nonconformists. Spurgeon himself had declared in favour of unsectarianism. In the thick of Down-Grade he had said, 'Oh, that the day would come when in a larger communion than any sect can offer, all those who are one in Christ may be able to blend in perfect unity.' Poole-Connor not only reacted against sectarianism, but also against modernism.

Notice was taken of him by the local ministers and Baptist hierarchy, once he showed *visibly* that he was making a success of his ministry. He supervised the building of the church and school and worked hard to get the money. The church flourished and the new building was filled. It was evidently time for others to pay attention to him. He studied for the Baptist Union examination, and passed with honours, but could not agree with the lectures. He wrote to the Union and protested against false doctrine. Pastor James Stephens, of Highgate Chapel, London, who became a lifelong friend, assisted him in his continuing studies. It was at this time of his life he developed his thinking on the question of evangelical unity.

Also about this time he was invited to a private meeting of Baptist ministers and theological college professors where the drift to higher criticism was discussed. Poole-Connor was alarmed to see for himself that it was welcomed by all, and the growing turmoil of his conscience, aching for years over this issue, could defer action no longer. 'At last I cut the bonds that bound me: I resigned my pastorate after ten years' work, and went to live at Twickenham to await God's leading.' This was his decisive departure from the compromised Baptist Union. The issue was too important to be delayed even until an Independent pastorate was offered him; his removal was an act of faith.

First he stayed with a wealthy aunt, and then for a few months a house was lent to him. He attended Amyand Park Chapel at Twickenham, where the Rev Jesse Sayer was pastor. Poole-Connor was a strict Sabbatarian, and he and his wife sometimes walked to Surbiton on the Lord's Day. Sabbath observance meant a great deal to the majority of English people. Gladstone had written some twenty years previously, 'It seems to be unquestionable that the observance of Sunday rest has taken deep root both in the convictions and the habits of the immense majority of my countrymen.' Things had not changed much since then.

At this time, just before World War I, churches continued to attract the people, and even grew numerically. Also, Nonconformists still had great influence in Parliament. And yet, a generalised spiritual apostasy progressed rapidly in the land as all the major denominations moved in the direction of higher criticism. As far as Nonconformists were concerned, Glover says that, 'a unanimous and uncompromising opposition to higher criticism might have called a strong conservative scholarship into being.'[4] This did not happen, and higher criticism speedily gained ground.

The Anglicans moved with equal speed, yet there was a solid group who remained loyal to the old views of the Bible. There was also conflict within the Presbyterian church in England over the introduction of a new creed. Evangelicals in this body tried to secure assent to the verbal inspiration of Scripture, but they failed. Laymen were slower to accept higher criticism than ministers, and the strong influence of laymen in the governing bodies of the Presbyterian church slowed down the progress of higher criticism. The leaders were very careful to avoid any controversy that might seriously split or weaken the church, so when, in 1890, they had to choose a new professor of Hebrew and Old Testament for the English Presbyterian College, they chose a man who espoused higher criticism, but had published no books on it, and possessed a 'warmly evangelistic spirit'. He was regarded as a safe man. The Methodists were slower than the other major denominations in adopting higher criticism, but when it did enter their ranks they were unprepared for it, and succumbed to it quickly.

Poole-Connor, writing later in *The Apostasy of English Nonconformity,* describes the scene after the death of Spurgeon: 'Spurgeon's efforts to stem the tide of modernism in the Nonconformist churches did little more than to show the strength of the current he opposed; and the proof of this is found in the swiftness and fullness with which that tide is running today. It is now our unwelcome task to show that this view is justified by facts.'

At this point, Poole-Connor turns his attention to an example of modernism in the person of A. S. Peake, biblical scholar and commentary writer. He proceeds:

'In the obituary article which appeared in *The Times* of August 20th, 1929, the significance of his career as a Free Churchman is specially dwelt upon. In the course of the article some illuminating facts emerge. Dr Peake was a Primitive Methodist, and although he belonged as such to a "community to whom the letter and authority of Scripture are especially dear", he "early in life grasped the importance of the higher criticism and never wavered in affirming it". In spite of his advocacy of higher criticism, he was a growing influence in his own religious community. He was elected President of the Free Church Council in the year preceding his death. The obituary article closes with the following statement, the importance of which will readily be seen: "Perhaps it was Dr Peake's greatest service, not merely to his own communion, but to the whole religious life of England, that he helped to save us from a fundamental controversy such as that which has devastated large sections of the church in America . . . If the Free Churches of England have been able without disaster to navigate the broken waters of the last thirty years, it is largely to the wisdom and patience of trusty and trusted pilots like Arthur Samuel Peake that they owe it."

'What, then, exactly *[Poole-Connor continues]*, was the doctrinal position of this "trusty and trusted pilot" of Nonconformity? He was a prolific writer, but, as the author of *The Times* article says, "the work by which he is best known and will, in all probability, be longest remembered, is the *Bible Commentary*, in one volume, which was published in 1919," for which he gathered round him a band of "admirable scholars", himself contributing the sections on *Genesis, Isaiah 1-39, Jonah, 1 Corinthians*, and some general articles. By this *Commentary*, then, his position may be fairly judged; and with it, the position of the English Free Churches, whom he so largely enabled "without disaster to navigate the broken waters of the last thirty years".

'Underlying all its expositions is a theory of so revolutionary a character as to render the remainder of the volume of little more importance than a treatise upon the opinions of the Early Fathers or the Jewish Rabbis. The theory in question concerns the seat of authority in religion. In dealing with the subject of authority in religion, the *Commentary* is quite candid. After the Reformation, it tells us, "Protestants fell back on the Book as the ultimate standard of religious Truth. Round this idea clustered a formidable set of affirmations regarding its inerrancy and its perfect consistency with itself . . . The rise of historical and linguistic criticism finally destroyed this claim."

'How final and thorough, in the eyes of the *Commentary*, was its destruction the following quotations will show: "In reading the Old Testament, we are not dealing with history at all, in the modern sense of the term; it lacks nearly all the notes of modern history. The writers knew nothing of history in the modern sense of the term; myth, legend, tradition, were all accepted without question. A simple historical fact (Jericho) has been altered out of all recognition. The author stated that what he thought ought to have occurred (Cities of Refuge) did as a fact, actually occur."

'As to the New Testament – "We are still far from having any proof that we have the *ipsissima verba** of Jesus, or any guarantee that the events of His life are related with absolute accuracy in the

---

*Latin – the precise words.

Gospels." Finally, of certain portions of the chapter in which the apostle Paul deals with the resurrection of the body, the *Commentary* says: "*[This is]* one of the most daring pieces of speculation."

'But if it can no longer be claimed that authority in religion is found in an inerrant Bible, where is it to be looked for? The *Commentary's* answer is as follows: "It still remains an incontestable, because experimental, truth, that out of the Bible a divine voice speaks; and when the accents of that divine voice come home to us we cannot for a moment doubt that we are face to face with the ultimate authority over the human soul. This is quite other than affirming the infallible authority of the Bible as a written revelation."'

From Peake as described by Poole-Connor, we pass to another leading figure of this period, Joseph Parker, the immensely popular minister of the City Temple in London. Parker was concerned about the progress of higher criticism, saying, 'There is a Bible dear to the common people . . . they were made by it, converted by it, and they live upon it, and I do not want the critics to take it away until they have something better to give than "a series of tentative suggestions" and the hope of finding some help in "future excavations".'[5] However, Parker failed to see the issues as clearly as C. H. Spurgeon. Unlike the latter, he kept up close associations with advanced critics, this clouding his judgement so much that he took the wrong side in the Down-Grade Controversy. Indeed, he attacked Spurgeon outrageously saying, 'You bring sweeping charges against your brethren for want of orthodoxy, but I will not join you in what may be anonymous defamation. I take another course. I say to you, "Thou art the man." I accuse you of the heterodoxy of onesidedness; I accuse you of want of spiritual discrimination; I accuse you of a bluntness which can only be accounted for by the worst kind of spiritual ignorance. The universe is not divided into plain black and white, as you suppose. It is not your function to set some people on your right hand, and the rest on your left. What if at the last the publicans and harlots should enter the kingdom of Heaven, and we ourselves should be shut out?

'You are inexcusably contemptuous in your views of authors who have forgotten more than you and I put together ever knew . . . You are also much too free in your excommunications. Believe me you are really not infallible . . . I almost tremble at my own temerity, for I cannot but think that any man who expels the whole Baptist Union must occupy a sovereign place in some pantheon of his own invention.'[6]

Parker was an evangelical, but how little doctrine meant to him is seen by the fact that he recommended R. J. Campbell as his successor at the City Temple, whose strong approval of higher criticism was well-known. Parker epitomised the popular evangelical who opened the door to higher criticism.

Having jettisoned the Bible the higher critics were in difficulties when it came to deciding what was the authority for religion. If the Bible was not infallibly true in all its parts, how could anyone know what was certainly right and from God? The problem of *authority* became a major issue. R. W. Dale had insisted on Christian experience as the authority, but this was inadequate, for Christianity rests on facts. P. T. Forsyth tried to solve this problem (anticipating Karl Barth's existentialism), writing: 'Nothing is revelation in the close use of words, which is not verifiable in our Christian experience. We have come up to date; people want to have experience without doctrine!' This was the new position – truth is what we feel to be true.

The most serious aspect of the decline was the apparent lack of conviction of men like Joseph Parker, who were generally considered to be stalwarts for the faith. Parker never adopted higher criticism, but his recommendation of R. J. Campbell as his successor is staggering. Glover tells us: 'Campbell became the pastor of City Temple in 1903 and the congregation became as attached to him as they had been to Parker. This illustrates the ease with which the adjustment to higher criticism was made.'[7] Here lies the key to the situation. What was the use of speaking against heresy if you hand over your people to a preacher who holds the very views you have just denounced? How much real conviction could he have imparted to his congregation, who became so attached to Campbell?

Such hypocrisy coming from such a quarter did far more harm than the 'new theology' Campbell was about to expound. Eli's weakness was more reprehensible than the abominable behaviour of his sons because he knew better. He rebuked, but did not restrain. Parker supported the men for whom the Truth of God was almost only an opinion. Other examples could be given of his approval of higher critics.

A. C. Underwood, having no great sympathy with C. H. Spurgeon, considers it would have been better for him – 'if he had mixed more with the great men of his time', adding, 'Joseph Parker hinted at this in an open letter which appeared in *The British Weekly*.'[8] To Parker, the theatre was quite all right, and so was society life generally. Spurgeon saw a vital difference between Parker's religion and his own. Both were great preachers, both highly respected, but represented two very different kinds of Christian. This was the evangelical scene immediately preceding Poole-Connor's ministry, the significance of which now deeply impressed itself upon him.

In his *Evangelicalism in England* Poole-Connor describes at length the case of Joseph Parker's successor, R. J. Campbell, and his 'new theology'. He gives abundant evidence to show how far he had moved from an evangelical position. He refers to Campbell's book, *The New Theology*:

'The most significant review of it was that found in the *Clarion*, the then organ of the Free-thought party. "Mr Campbell is a Christian minister and I am an infidel editor; and the difference between his religion and mine is too small to be worth arguing about . . .

Mr Campbell believes – I think – in immortality. I have no data on the subject. Mr Campbell calls nature, God; I call nature, nature. Mr Campbell thinks we ought to have some form of supernatural religion, associated with Christ; I prefer the religion of humanity. Mr Campbell thinks Jesus the most perfect man that ever lived; I think otherwise. Beyond these differences, I am as much a Christian as Rev R. J. Campbell, and the Rev R. J. Campbell is as much an infidel as the Editor of the *Clarion* . . . He rejects the doctrine of the Fall and of the atonement; he denies the divinity of Christ, the virgin birth, and the resurrection; he denies the inspiration and infallibility of the Bible, and he rejects the idea of divine punishment and an everlasting hell. So do I. He abandons the orthodox theory of sin; he says that selfishness is sin, and that unselfishness is morality and salvation. So do I." '

Poole-Connor adds, very perceptively, 'That such teaching should be heard in the Christian pulpit, and should obtain a large measure of acceptance, is no new thing; nor is it, viewed from one standpoint, an occasion for great alarm. What is of importance is the reaction to it on the part of those having oversight of the body to which the teacher belongs. Mr Campbell's aberrations caused the Congregational Union much perturbation. Its more orthodox members were hampered by the traditional readiness of Independents to receive new ideas, and their refusal to "hedge the ministry with illiberal restrictions"; while some of its leaders, like Dr Horton (aided from outside by Dr Clifford), showed a measure of sympathy with the City Temple preacher's views. When therefore the matter came to an issue at a meeting held on June 9th, 1910, the Union declined to take any decisive step.'

In spite of these astounding compromises, the nation was still not far from the times when God's Word had been preached with revival power. The tremendous momentum generated fifty years previously still carried people to church, even though doctrines were being undermined. The number of people who attended church was still rising. It took two terrible wars to reveal that the essential life had gone out of the churches. Then the autumn leaves were suddenly blown away by two great gales, leaving scarcely anything behind. The life had gone from the churches in the period we have under review.

During this period there was certainly great activity amongst evangelicals, almost as though evangelistic activity could take the place of resisting modernism in their ranks. As they faced the great changes, they concentrated their effort in organisations and movements outside the life of the churches. This tended to obscure the real declension, and give an appearance of success by virtue of the growth of the various movements.

At this time came another wave of evangelistic campaigns from the USA. The place of D. L. Moody as the leading revivalist was taken at his death by Dr R. A. Torrey. The term 'revivalist' is used deliberately, since Torrey considered that, 'A revival ought to be the normal condition of the church of Christ, and not merely a spasmodic outburst.' His biographer adds, 'Dr Torrey has lived in a constant revival. In every one of his four pastorates he has had a constant revival.'[9]

This attitude towards revival marks a clear change in the understanding and usage of the term. Poole-Connor often spoke on the subject. It was a most vital subject with him throughout his life, particularly in his latter years. To him a revival was a 'visitation of grace', not the 'normal condition of the church of Christ'. Doubtless he would have agreed that a church should experience tokens of divine favour, and be spiritually alive at all times, but when he used the term 'revival' he was describing an event that by its remarkable nature (and purpose) could not be continuous, neither *has been*, historically.

In April, 1907, he wrote an article entitled, 'Ordinary and

Extraordinary'. In this he complained that: 'Very frequently, the words "mission" and "revival" are used as if they were interchangeable terms. Yet there is so great a difference between the two as to demand a most careful distinction in employing them. And the distinction is deeper than mere words. The confusion of a mission with a revival is far worse than bad etymology; it is bad theology. It is not only that the root idea of the word "mission" is that of "being sent", and the root idea of the word "revival" that of "living afresh"; there is as great a difference between the things themselves. A mission represents the ordinary work of the Christian church; a revival is an extraordinary work of God.

'For a mission *is* simply an effort on the part of the church to bring the Gospel to bear upon the world. It is the recognition that as Jesus Christ was sent by God into the world, so the church is sent by Jesus Christ into the world. And this should be the normal attitude of every church. There may be occasions when special efforts are made, when men who can preach the Gospel interestingly, and in language understood of the people, are called to help. But so long as there is a man who has not had the possibility of salvation presented to him, so long the church's work remains unfinished.'

Attention has been drawn to Dr Torrey's notion of revival because it emphasises the change that was developing in the understanding of many evangelicals as to what a revival really was, and what they were praying for when they uttered the words, 'Revive Thy work, O Lord.'

Torrey was a man of intellectual stature. When he came to London for meetings held under the auspices of the National Free Church Council, he unashamedly declared his creed. This was at a time when creeds were despised by many, and when modernism was at its height. He declared his belief in the basic fundamentals of the faith: 'I do not find one ray of hope held out by Christ to those who die without accepting Christ in the life that now is.' On verbal inspiration he was not so distinct, but made allowances for those who held different theories of inspiration. This was a pity, in view of the need for this particular doctrine to be stated plainly at the time.

Torrey shared Moody's sincerity and directness, and his ministry was in great demand over the whole English-speaking world. Charles Alexander, the singer, accompanied Torrey on his London mission, this being a gigantic affair. 'Used as it is to things on a gigantic scale, there is something in this revival movement that even the Metropolis has never witnessed. Nothing like it has ever been planned before. There have been missions and missions, but this one is unique. It stands alone.'[10]

On the opening night the audience was in silent expectation. Alexander offered a prayer 'that these songs may be sung all over London, so that thousands may be sung into the kingdom of God'. 'These people must be made to sing,' was the dominant thought with Alexander. 'I just felt,' he said to his biographer afterwards, 'that I must make the people sing, and I forgot everything else. I felt that they must sing.'

The hymn, 'Oh, it is wonderful', quickly captivated the vast throng. The singing proceeded, and 'all were doing their best to please. Every motion of the conductor was obeyed with soldier-like precision.' Later, Alexander sang as a solo, 'Tell mother I'll be there'. It was dramatically sung, and had a powerful effect upon the audience. London received the first night with a great welcome, and the papers without exception praised it. Alexander's conducting, in particular, was remarked on. 'London likes new sensations, and I predict that London will go crazy over Alexander the Great. Alexander is more than a choir conductor. He is a crowd conductor. He will make London hum, for he will make London sing.'[11]

Three honoured and trusted Christian leaders, Prebendary Webb-Peploe, Dr F. B. Meyer and Dr Campbell Morgan, were present, and the expression on their countenances convinced Alexander's biographer (who observed them carefully) that they, like the others, enjoyed and approved the proceedings. At the time, Poole-Connor, along with others, could not see the danger. He was then ministering at Surbiton, and so heard Torrey preach and Alexander sing as he had heard Moody preach and Sankey sing. He attended the great opening meeting in the company of Dr F. B. Meyer, who had shared in the opening service of the new church at Surbiton. He would not at this stage have known about Torrey's neutrality on verbal inspiration, and does not appear to have reacted negatively to the evangelist's inclination to crowd-manipulation.

During the first part of the 20th century great energy was put by Christians into two movements – the promotion of special evangelistic campaigns, and the promotion of special meetings for sanctification, known as the holiness movement. Very little attention was paid to the doctrinal problem, and particularly the undermining of biblical inerrancy and authority. While these two movements drew together evangelicals from different denominations, they bypassed the real problem of compromise. For a time it did not seem to matter, but while evangelicals were active in their movements, modernists were active in the churches, changing and fashioning the machinery of government. Modernists were concerned to make the 'management' machinery efficient, while evangelicals were concerned with securing conversions and commitments by means of their movements.

The three older Nonconformist bodies (the Presbyterians, Congregationalists and Baptists) evolved greater centralisation in these years. John Howard Shakespeare, while Secretary of the Baptist Union (1898-1924), managed to increase the power of the Union enormously, while the various Methodist groupings began to unite together. The vacuum created by the rejection of the doctrines of the Word of God was increasingly filled by the ecumenical movement. Evangelicals seemingly showed no interest in the growing

control of the denominations by modernists. Their two great preoc-
cupations were to get great numbers to 'decide for Christ', and also
to accept what was presented in holiness meetings – the idea of
'sanctification by faith' – and this was pursued using stereotyped
emotional methods.

In 1910, Poole-Connor was invited by Fuller Gooch, of West
Norwood, London to join him as assistant-pastor, a move which
shaped further his vision for the uniting of evangelical believers who
turned their back on modernism.

Poole-Connor refers to the character of Fuller Gooch's church –
Lansdowne Hall – at length in *Evangelical Unity*: It was 'the
memorial to a strong man's convictions, to which, after thirty-three
years of denominational ministry, he felt impelled to give unfettered
expression.' It was in the fullest sense an evangelical and unsectarian
Christian assembly. The form of government which its founder
regarded as being most scriptural was that of a modified Presbyteri-
anism, or oversight of the flock by elders. Baptism by immersion
was taught and administered, but agreement with this was not made
a condition of membership. Mr Gooch's belief that the undenominational position was closest to the New Testament pattern did not
prevent his maintaining cordial relations with members of the evangelical denominations; and clergymen and Free Church ministers
who were 'sound in faith' were alike heartily received.

While at Lansdowne Hall, Poole-Connor's keen discernment of
events in the church at large was further sharpened. Fuller Gooch
hoped that he would remain for many years, and be his successor,
but he only stayed for two. His preaching was found to be so acceptable that it created embarrassment. Fuller Gooch drew large
companies, but the younger man found his own acceptability a
problem, and resigned to avoid a developing strain in the church.
He could not bear the thought of division. Once more he left a fruitful sphere of labour, 'not knowing whither he went'. He had no call

to any other place at the time, and this was not an easy situation, there being at that time so few Independent churches.

His departure from Lansdowne Hall was a terrible disappointment to some, who later moved to North Kensington so that they could enjoy his next ministry at Talbot Tabernacle, Bayswater. The Tabernacle owned a house in North Kensington, where the Poole-Connors went to live and an elder from Lansdowne moved to a house opposite. Poole-Connor discouraged Lansdowne members from doing this, but such was his popularity that some would not be put off.

At about this time a general concern at last developed among Nonconformists over the state of their churches. Suddenly, numbers were not increasing, and it was becoming obvious that their spiritual condition was at a low ebb. Andrew Murray wrote a book in 1911, entitled *The State of the Church*, in which he describes this widespread concern. What is particularly noticeable is that there was scarcely any recognition of the principal cause of the trouble. Murray refers approvingly to the World Missionary Conference held in Edinburgh, in 1910 (the start of the modern ecumenical movement) and the alarm expressed there at the lethargic condition of the churches.

Murray quotes from one of the conference statements, 'We must make men understand that it is only their lack of faith and half-hearted consecration that hinders the rapid advance of the work; only their own coldness that keeps back His redemption.' He takes up the point of 'consecration', and pursues it throughout the rest of the book, and uses expressions such as 'full surrender' and 'abundant life' scores of times. He keeps saying precisely the same thing in a variety of different ways. He was convinced that the 'secret' of success, and the 'key' to the situation was the need for an act of dedication. There is a reference to statements made at the conference that 'higher criticism had much to do with loss of power in the preaching, and the lack of an earnest Christian life,' but in his own treatment of the situation it was to him almost irrelevant.

How tragic that such a man as he could not see the seriousness of the apostasy, and when writing a book that dealt specifically with 'The State of the Church', scarcely referred to higher criticism. When he did, he merely quoted others briefly, and added no comment. However, Murray was simply presenting the current favoured formula for curing spiritual ills. The connection between the defence of the Word of God and the blessing of the Holy Spirit was ignored. But how could there be any improvement when the cause itself was not recognised by eminent evangelical leaders?

Only here and there did individuals draw the connection between higher criticism and the decline of spirituality – Poole-Connor being one of the few. He had himself commented on 'the present spiritual drought' four years previously, while still at Surbiton: 'It was our lot,' he recorded, 'to attend the Autumn Meetings of the Home Counties' Baptist Association, and the question put down for the afternoon conference was "The Present Spiritual Drought". The Rev E. H. Brown indicated the present position of the Baptist Church in this country by giving us the statistics of the majority of the County Associations. The impression left on the mind was that the great bulk of Associations reported actual decrease in membership, and the remainder an insignificant increase. Then the Rev E. W. Tarbox dealt with the cause of this condition of things. He had noticed, he said, that at the period when the views of Scripture usually associated with higher criticism began to take hold of the churches of this country, then definite cases of conversion began to decrease. In proportion to the lowering of the church's estimate of the Scriptures, there had been a lowering of the tone of spiritual life. All this, in his view, had created an atmosphere antagonistic to conversion, and in this atmosphere the faithful churches suffered with the unfaithful . . .

'We avow our concurrence in Mr Tarbox's suggestion that the innocent suffer with the guilty, and that a general low spiritual tone acts adversely on all the churches. Caleb and Joshua, who "wholly followed the Lord", were kept out of their inheritance for forty years because of Israelitish unbelief. But Caleb and Joshua were preserved, and entered upon their inheritance at last. Only let us see that we are right with God, are wholly faithful to Him, and sooner or later the inheritance shall be ours.'

By 1911, Poole-Connor was much occupied with the subject of evangelical unity, based on loyalty to the inerrant Scriptures, as opposed to loyalty to a denomination. The seed was in his mind, and was beginning to grow. It was clear to him from history, as well as from the Word, that the binding together of sheep and goats by professing loyalty to a 'secondary' issue (such as the mode of baptism) as practised in the denominations, had hastened doctrinal decline. Like Caleb, Poole-Connor outlived his generation, and was able to use his faculties to the very end. He also sought to form a body that did not partake of men's heresies. This, alas, was no more successful in the long run than previous attempts to form a 'pure body', but for a time it flourished and proved a blessing.

Notes

1   G. R. Balleine, *History of the Evangelical Party in the Church of England*, Longman, Green & Co., London, 1933, p. 236.
2   *Our Churches and Why We Belong to Them*, Service and Paton, 1898, p. 370.
3   A. H. Stockwell, *The Baptist Churches of Surrey*, 1910 – from the section by E. J. Poole-Connor.
4   W. B. Glover, *Evangelical Nonconformists and Higher Criticism in the 19th Century*, Independent Press, London, 1954, p. 185.
5   Glover, ibid., p. 226.
6   Glover, ibid., p. 245.
7   Glover, ibid., p. 246.
8   A. C. Underwood, *A History of the English Baptists*, Carey Kingsgate, London, 1947.
9   J. K. Maclean, *Torrey and Alexander*, S. W. Partridge & Co., London, p. 32.
10 Maclean, ibid., p. 84.
11 Maclean, ibid., p. 89.

7

Talbot Tabernacle and Beyond

THE YEAR 1914 ushered in an era in which Satan was permitted to exercise increasingly his terrible power. For decades Britain felt the effects of that disaster known as the Great War, when so many lives were lost. Conscription was not introduced until well into the war, so that a large proportion of those lost were perhaps the most courageous members of society. A considerable portion of the volunteers were Nonconformists, who were frequently given directions to join up from the pulpits. Nonconformist churches lost the best of an entire generation.

The popular view that man was improving morally by the improvement of his environment had become almost universal, and most people expected the 20th century to be the golden age. Until World War I there had been no large-scale war for nearly a hundred years. The Great War, unlike the Second World War, came suddenly, and its vast scale shocked almost everyone. Horne's *Popular History of the Free Churches* expressed the view that: 'the War caught the Free Churches in this country napping, as it caught most Christians. Too easily we had assumed that the spread of education and the growth of commerce had made war impossible, that all civilised nations had too much common sense to settle their quarrels in so barbarous and primitive a way.'[1]

Poole-Connor was pastoring at Talbot Tabernacle, Bayswater, during the whole of the First World War (his first pastorate there), and for most of the Second (his second pastorate there). He had left Lansdowne Hall 'not knowing whither he went', but he did not have to wait long. A few weeks after resigning from Lansdowne, he was invited to Talbot Tabernacle, an Independent church in Bayswater, west-central London. He describes the history of the Tabernacle briefly in *Evangelical Unity*. He refers to the fact that it was a direct offspring of the 1859 Revival, a large iron building being initially erected which would house the growing unsectarian church for nearly twenty years. The first pastor went to Australia, and Frank H. White, a student at C. H. Spurgeon's Pastors' College, was called in his stead. Under his much-blessed ministry the handsome buildings were erected in 1888, Lord Shaftesbury and Sir George Williams laying the foundation stones, and C. H. Spurgeon preaching a dedicatory sermon. Dr Tom Barnardo and Rev F. B. Meyer were among the speakers at the opening service.

Poole-Connor's thumbnail history of the Talbot Tabernacle gives a further reminder of the scale of blessing still experienced in the second part of the 19th century. He says this of the second pastor:

'Mr White was a man of gracious personality and a true pastor. In his prime the large building *[it held 1,000]* was filled to its utmost capacity; and late-comers would often be told to go to the adjoining parish church "as they would hear the same Gospel there". Mr White fostered missionary interests and evangelistic zeal. He secured funds to purchase a former public house and made it a mission hall. He was a firm yet gracious "defender of the faith", and strongly supported Mr Spurgeon in his Down-Grade protest. His pastorate at the Tabernacle closed in 1906, although until his death some nine years later he held an honoured place in the hearts of all the church members, and was a frequent and welcome visitor.'

Poole-Connor was welcomed as pastor in January, 1913. An article in *The Christian* in February 1914, provides an interesting commentary on the Tabernacle, and on this phase of his life:

'Among the great centres of Christian activity which abound in and around London, a large place must be given to some which stand out from the rest as separated and isolated units, but which nevertheless count for much in the sum total of the work of the one church of Christ. Prominent among these interdenominational and unsectarian churches are the Metropolitan Tabernacle, in the southeast; the East London Tabernacle, the Great Assembly Hall, and the Edinburgh Castle, in the east; and the Talbot Tabernacle in the west.'

The article goes on to speak of Poole-Connor's ministry: 'As a preacher, Mr Poole-Connor is singularly gifted. A lifelong and earnest study of the Word has resulted not only in a well-furnished mind, but in a passionate love for the Bible and for the Christ of the Bible. Preaching is his supreme delight. Having secured his subject by prayerful dependence upon the Spirit's guidance, and having mastered it by diligent study, he delivers his message extemporaneously, and with perfect naturalness; passing from point to point with much ease and directness, and all the while revelling in the privilege of proclaiming such a "glorious Gospel". As an expositor of the Word in its deeper aspects, Mr Poole-Connor is finding his rightful place. Prolonged study of the prophetic portions of the Bible, and of the vital subject of our Lord's return, has brought him into singular agreement with the well-known view of his venerable predecessors.'

When Poole-Connor began at Talbot Tabernacle the membership

was a little over 300, but with far higher attendances. A very slight loss over his eight year (first) pastorate was considered an achievement, as the very dramatic fall in church attendance in England had begun. The Sunday School at the Tabernacle was very large, for spread across the church and its branch mission at Talbot Hall there were 650 children, a figure that rose to 1,000 over the next ten years.

The article in *The Christian* tells of an additional Monday prayer meeting for foreign missions; of systematic visitation in the district; of open-air meetings held every week; and of a winter soup-kitchen for the poor. The article also refers to the changes that had taken place since the Tabernacle had been built in 1888, for then Notting Hill was a well-to-do residential neighbourhood, but the whole district had changed as the handsome houses with imposing porticos, once occupied by prosperous merchants and professional people, had been turned into flats. The need for a faithful and aggressive Gospel ministry in such a locality had become increasingly urgent, and the task of maintaining such a work had become correspondingly difficult.

William Horsburgh was a schoolboy when he first saw and heard Poole-Connor. 'He made a deep impression on my immature mind, which remained unclouded and undimmed for nearly fifty long years. My first remembrance of him is of a neat dapper figure in a morning coat, then in his early forties, with a clear voice, fresh and vigorous in speaking, yet with a quiet dignity which remained with him all through the years. Even those of us who were young in years could listen with full interest and understanding to his expository preaching. His rich insight into scriptural Truth, especially the Old Testament and typology, and his gracious ability to throw fresh light on old and familiar passages, made his ministry fragrant to us all. Indeed, his unique gifts as a preacher were ever an example, and throughout his long life we were blessed by his encouragement and keen interest in our own Christian witness . . .

'He was also a Father Confessor to many of us. We did not always obtain "absolution" from him, but when we consulted him in our earliest days, and throughout the years, with our hopes and our fears, our failings and our forebodings, he always had the right word of guidance, comfort, hope, and maybe of gentle rebuke. A private audience with our Pastor was an assurance of being lifted up out of the depths. He was a great listener, sympathetic and gentle, and so intensely interested in all that we were doing. In our intimacy with him we knew some of his sorrows and heartaches. He was ever humble in his manner and deportment, and few outside his intimate circle could have known how heavy were his burdens at times. He seemed to have an infinite capacity for suffering.'

The *Year Book* of the Tabernacle for 1915 gives a picture of the life of the church in the most testing of times. The pastor introduces the report with a review of the previous year:

'The year 1914 will be known as the year in which the most terrible war in the history of the world broke out, and the church at Talbot Tabernacle in common with all other assemblies of God's people has been considerably affected thereby. Some of our younger brethren have joined the army, thus depleting our staff of workers, while others are serving as special constables. Indeed, conditions in general have been such as to call for the exercise of faith and endurance. Nevertheless, by the grace of God, a truly Christian spirit has been exhibited. Parents have entrusted their beloved sons, who have responded to their country's call, to God's care, with quiet confidence and submission.

'Some associated with us have lost those dear to them on the field of battle; yet in their sorrow they have not "charged God foolishly". Brethren whose temporal affairs have been adversely affected, have maintained an attitude of cheerful trust. Many who have had previously occasion to say "The Lord gave", and now have to say "the Lord hath taken away", have had grace to add "and blessed be the name of the Lord". But notwithstanding all these things the work has been well sustained.'

During that year Poole-Connor received thirty-eight people into membership; thirteen by baptism, eighteen by profession, and seven by transfer – those by baptism coming chiefly from the Sunday Schools. Their membership, after drastic revision of the church roll, stood at 323, an entirely realistic figure. The Sunday Schools, as noted already, totalled about 650 children, while all over the country the numbers were steadily declining. The Tabernacle took an interest in about twenty missionary societies (especially the China Inland Mission, North Africa Mission and Mildmay Mission), and had eight members serving abroad as missionaries at this time.

Poole-Connor gave particular emphasis to the second coming, and in a short book entitled, *The Coming of the Son of Man*, which was reprinted twice, the author wrote: 'This little book is intended for the use of beginners in the study of the Scriptures concerning the Lord's return. It is entirely non-controversial, and no reference is made, therefore, to other views. The writer, however, is not unacquainted with them.'

This writer, though holding a view of prophecy that is different from that of Poole-Connor, found scarcely anything he could not agree with. In chapter 5 of his book – 'The Lord's Coming in Relation to the Believer's Service' – he warned in these words against a false attitude towards the return of Christ:

'Here is the true perspective of the Lord's coming and here its true power. The motive for holiness of life and for earnestness of labour is found, not in a fear that the Lord may stealthily come and catch His servants momentarily off duty, but in a solemn conviction that all our days of service must be accounted for to Him; that whether our lot be resurrection or translation, our lives shall equally be subjected to the scrutiny of Him whose eyes are like a flame of fire, and that in proportion to our fidelity there shall be, in ways but obscurely revealed at present, certain reward or certain loss.'

For him the event was not simply the thrilling moment when God would intervene in history, but the very goal and aim of his life, the completion of God's redemptive purpose for him – glorification. It made him seek to live a holy life, rather than to try to fit the events he read in the newspaper into prophecy and work out how near the end might be. Poole-Connor's ministry was truly an 'all-round' one, and the church could accurately be described as a light shining brightly amidst the gloom of spiritual twilight.

During this period theological liberalism, the complete rejection of an inspired Bible and the denial of essential evangelical doctrines, which was the inevitable outcome of higher criticism, reached its most atheistic form. So-called 'fundamentalism' was a protest against this form of atheism. In the United States the conflict was sharper than in Britain for two reasons. The liberals in the USA were more extreme in their statements, and a larger proportion of evangelicals proved faithful and able in opposing them. The nearest development in Britain to the fundamentalist split in the USA was the formation of societies that were both fundamentalist and inter-denominational, one of the most important being the Inter-Varsity Fellowship, founded in 1919 (although we are bound to say that it had lost its original, militantly evangelical stance by the 1970s). Within the denominations some moves were made to form groups that were distinctively evangelical. In 1922 the Bible Churchman's Missionary Society was formed among Anglicans. Other missionary societies were formed with an evangelical basis of faith and an inter-denominational outlook. The prevailing liberalism was so bad that it produced this reaction.

Hindsight shows that all these promising reactions were really a side-stepping of the real problem facing evangelicals in the churches, namely involvement with false teachers. However, they certainly represented a realisation that evangelicals can only carry out evangelism with other evangelicals. Some individual congregations went further, adopting the principle of separation from those who denied the Gospel, and seeking fellowship exclusively with those who were truly evangelical. Already there were undenominational churches like the Talbot Tabernacle, but now a growing number of independent congregations came into being. To add to their ranks, a number of Baptist churches exercised their right to secede from the Baptist Union, thus following Spurgeon's example years before. Liberalism was a terrible scourge, but it could at least be responded to.

Despite such good reactions to liberalism, British evangelicals generally did not seize the opportunity to defend their position, as many did in the United States.

In 1921 Poole-Connor was called to a yet wider sphere of service when invited to become full-time Deputation Secretary for the North Africa Mission. During his first period with the mission, God brought him face to face with a great need in England, for the role led him into contact with Christians all over the country, and he gained considerable insight into the needs of the churches. He tells us in *Evangelical Unity* that: 'in traversing the country I acquired a considerable knowledge of its religious condition. I naturally took special interest in what I saw of the unattached churches. I found that the smaller assemblies of this order were often very isolated, some of them being scarcely aware that any others existed. I noted that many of their pastors, although spiritually qualified men, had no general recognition as accredited "ministers of religion". I observed that others, although being blessed to the conversion of the unsaved, were limited in their ability to "feed the flock of God", for lack of adequate training. On the other hand, I discovered that the Superintendents of the larger mission halls were usually men of marked ability, both as preachers and organisers, and that their congregations were often Independent evangelical churches in all but name. 'I also met a number of denominational ministers who were becoming disturbed at the growth of modernism in the body to which they belonged, but, being aware of the disagreeable consequences of secession, were uncertain as to the course to pursue.

'In all these cases there seemed to be either needs requiring to be met, or possibilities that might be developed; and the knowledge of them drove me to thought and prayer. Could not these unattached churches – so I began to ask myself – be brought together in some association of mutual helpfulness? Could not the men, evidently called of God to the pastoral office, whose names were in no denominational handbook, receive some other form of recognition? Could not the less scholarly brethren, whose call seemed equally evident, be helped to make up their educational leeway? Could not ministers that had left denominational unions at least be shown brotherly sympathy, and if they had lost their place on an accredited list, have another provided? It certainly seemed very desirable.

'Yet the problem was bristling with difficulties. The most formidable was the fact that any movement of the kind which largely affected undenominational churches would almost certainly be regarded as an effort to form a new sect – and one particularly open to objection. I foresaw the derisive tone criticism would take: "What do these feeble Jews? What is this ridiculous self-contradictory undenominational denomination?" it would be asked . . .

'I began to observe, as a fact which had a practical bearing on the subject, that sectarian divisions amongst the leading evangelical bodies arose not so much from differences on fundamental doctrines, as from divergent opinions concerning church government and church ordinances. Episcopalian, Presbyterian, Congregationalist, Baptist – each designation bears witness to varying views as to how the church's affairs should be managed or its ordinances administered. If the conflicting conclusions in regard to these two points . . . could be eliminated, the way would be paved for evangelicals to form one large, united and powerful church. This being the case – so the thought began to develop in my mind – why should not some simple organisation be formed to meet the present need, which could include all the unattached sections of Nonconformity, and from which these secondary questions should be excluded? Why should not some doctrinal basis acceptable to all its evangelical constituents be made the bond of fellowship, becoming the external symbol of a common inward experience of the saving power of Christ?

'I therefore approached a number of unsectarian churches and ministers – for I was bound to begin with these – and suggested that "a federation of undenominational and unattached churches, missions, and ministers, be formed". The use of the word "federation" was unfortunate. In spite of my disclaimer, it was taken by some to imply the very thing I was anxious to avoid – a proposal to form some new kind of sect. I had many rebuffs!'

Nevertheless, many supported Poole-Connor and he pressed forward. So, in 1922, the Fellowship of Undenominational and Unattached Churches and Missions was formed. He wrote a letter to *The Christian* in 1925 to explain the nature of this Fellowship of unattached churches, and to enlist further support:

'Dear Sir, Reference was made in your column some time ago to a proposal to draw the undenominational and unattached churches and missions into closer relationship. Sufficient time has now elapsed for it to be possible to report progress with some degree of definiteness. The proposal was on the whole warmly welcomed. On the ground of expediency alone, many felt it to be desirable that a responsible body of persons should compile and issue a register of undenominational and unattached churches and missions, and draw up a ministerial list, so that bona-fide pastors of churches and others should not be in danger of a loss of status in the eyes of the law as a result of their being outside denominational connections. It was found that, during the late war, the fact of being the pastor of a church was not always sufficient for recognition as a "Minister of Religion" by the authorities – reference to a "list" was also required.

'On the higher ground of what was felt to be the interests of Christian Truth, the proposal was also welcomed. Many were of the opinion that if some such union as was proposed was formed, with a strong "fundamentalist" basis, it would not only lessen the sense of isolation which many experience, but would also strengthen their hands in combating the dangers of modernism.

'A few regarded the project with hesitance. There was the quite natural fear to some lest another small sect should be formed, and an "undenominational denomination" (dreadful name!) should add to the confusions of religion. There was also the fear that such a union might itself degenerate and fresh secession be demanded. *[Sadly, this proved to be the case after nearly fifty years of faithful witness – DGF.]* Some holding strong views on baptism could not see their way to unite, even in a broad fellowship, with those who did not follow their mode of administration. Others even felt isolation itself to be a more scriptural position; while a final difficulty was to find a credal basis at once exclusive and inclusive enough to meet the case. Those expressing doubt, however, were greatly in the minority, and as the result of responses to the proposal, the "Fellowship of Undenominational and Unattached Churches and Missions" was formed, a strongly fundamentalist credal basis agreed upon, and a register of churches, missions, pastors and evangelists (now in its second year) duly commenced. The Fellowship will shortly be legally incorporated.'

This was the formula for association between congregations which was to serve well for many years, namely, whatever the distinctive doctrines or practices of a church may be, fellowship between them required only the wholehearted acceptance of the inspired Word and the central doctrines of the Gospel. It could not be seen, in the

1920s, that a new set of dangers would begin to present themselves in the 1960s, which would render the formula ineffective.

Poole-Connor later wrote: 'The membership steadily increased. Sufficient money was secured to have the Fellowship legally incorporated. Later, when it had thoroughly found its feet, its Articles of Association were revised and strengthened by permission of the Board of Trade, and its title changed from "The Fellowship of Undenominational and Unattached Churches and Missions" to "The Fellowship of Independent Evangelical Churches".'

After eight years as Deputation Secretary with the North Africa Mission, at the age of 57, Poole-Connor returned to the pastorate, briefly serving the Walker Memorial Church at Cheltenham, but he greatly missed being in London, as he was involved with many societies, and served on various committees.

Returning to the North Africa Mission as General Secretary, his family moved to Highgate Hill. A mission officer wrote: 'As General Secretary of the NAM he was a beloved colleague at headquarters, an able grappler with field problems, the very oil of grace that makes a council meeting move smoothly, and a clear and able writer on Muslim themes.' It was while he was General Secretary of the NAM that his wisdom and far-sightedness were responsible for a most important development in the work at Tangier, Morocco. The old Mission Hospital in that rapidly growing cosmopolitan city was desperately behind the times in equipment, amenities and accommodation. Through Poole-Connor's advocacy and zeal, help was speedily forthcoming on a truly lavish scale. An excellent new wing was added to the Tulloch Memorial Hospital, and a fine home built for the Medical Superintendent. A mission property had its upper storey rebuilt, and the whole structure was repaired and redecorated to become a nurses' home and guest house. The latter was certainly a window on North Africa, through which many a Christian traveller became an eyewitness of the missionary hospital's practical demonstration of the love of Christ to needy Muslims. Poole-Connor himself made many visits to North Africa in the service of the mission. His great burden for the area being seen in one of his compositions, 'A Prayer for North Africa':

O Lord our God, whose lofty throne
    The nations of the earth commands,
Assert Thy right, Thy power make known,
    Throughout great Afric's northern lands.

Bid Egypt heed Thy voice once more,
    And Libya hearken and obey;
Yea, speak until the utmost shore
    Of Mauritania owns Thy sway.

Regard Thine ancient heritage
    By alien feet long trodden down,
Her sins forgive, her griefs assuage,
    And all her toils with triumph crown.

We crave no conquest of the sword,
    A nobler victory would we gain;
O Spirit of the living Lord
    Come Thou and breathe upon the slain!

Awake the conscience; give the sense
    Of guilt and helplessness and loss,
Till through the tears of penitence
    Men see the glory of the Cross.

Notes

1   C. S. Horne, *Popular History of the Free Churches*, James Clarke & Co., London, 1903, p. 445.

8

Times of Steepening Decline

THE MOST REMARKABLE and discerning insight into the great evangelical decline ever penned is unquestionably Poole-Connor's masterpiece – *The Apostasy of English Nonconformity*. It appeared in 1933, providing an absorbing commentary both on the times and on his own convictions. In his introduction he lays bare the scene, expressing how baffled he was that no amount of unbelief expressed by denominational leaders could strain the allegiance of evangelicals to these bodies. With evident heartbreak, he writes:

'One of the most disquieting features of the present religious situation in England is the attitude of conservative evangelical Nonconformists toward the form of teaching known as modernism. In view of their historic claim to speak their minds freely, it would have been thought impossible that they should permit their denominational leaders to foster principles that are so largely the negation of the older faith without some vigorous protest. Equally difficult would it have been to believe that they could, with apparent cordiality, co-operate with those who not only controvert their most cherished convictions, but often do so in terms of abuse and derision.

'Yet the majority of evangelicals associated with the Free Churches seem to be able to do both . . . The various unions and assemblies are still loyally supported and the numerous funds well supplied. Ministers, trained in colleges in which the older evangelicalism finds little or no place, are just as enthusiastically inducted; and deacons, who once loved to hear a far other type of preaching, still officiate. Here and there a voice is raised in protest; an occasional and little-heeded secession takes place; some Bible Unions are formed; but beyond this the evangelicals of organised Nonconformity scarcely lift a finger to show their disapproval.

'It need scarcely be said that this attitude constitutes a very real danger to the evangelical cause. It can only be construed by the rising generation, for example, in one of two ways. Either they will believe that those who profess the older faith hold it so lightly that it is to them a matter of indifference whether the contrary doctrines are taught or not; or else that there is so little essential difference between the two that their divergence is mainly a question of terminology. They will conclude that in either case nothing really matters. Yet for issues not one whit more serious than those which face the evangelicals of today, their forefathers surrendered almost all they held most dear, and "went out, not knowing whither they went".

'How is this attitude to be accounted for? A complete answer is probably impossible – so varied and complex are the springs of action. Denominational loyalty or partiality may be the reason with some. Fear of consequences may weigh with others. With others again it may be the result of a calculated policy. But in many cases the cause must surely be ignorance of facts. The majority cannot know what denominational leaders really hold or what the Nonconformist colleges – those institutions that control so largely Free Church theology – are actually teaching. No other reason seems adequate to explain their indifference to a change in religious thought so radical in character and so far-reaching in effects. *It is to assist in dissipating this ignorance and to plead for an attitude more worthy of the past that these pages are written.' [Italics mine – DGF.]*

The indictment is devastating, but, we believe, correct. Poole-Connor proceeds to show how this situation came about in the chapters that follow, showing, for example, how Baptist leader Dr Reaveley Glover was regarded by evangelicals, in spite of his modernism:

'In 1925 Dr Reaveley Glover became President of the Baptist Union. Commenting on his presidential address, the late Dr Fullerton *[a fervent evangelical]* wrote: "Even the most conservative of us but thanked God for such a man and such a message; none of us felt inclined to slay this prophet whom God had sent us . . . Instead, we took our leader to our hearts and under his guidance look for a year of deepening loyalty to the historic faith."'

Poole-Connor comments: 'That Dr Glover has the support of the modernist section of the Baptist body goes without saying; the words quoted above show that he has also the approval of its more conservative members; for, as the *Keswick Week* issued just prior to his death assured us, "there was no modernism about Dr Fullerton". The Rev R. B. Jones, it is true, protested against Dr Glover's appointment to the presidency of the Union, as did some others: nevertheless, on his election as Vice-President (preparatory to his automatic entry upon the higher office) he polled more votes than were ever before given to any nominee.'

Poole-Connor then deals with Glover's views: 'In common with many occupying a similar theological position, Dr Glover often writes in a very confusing manner. He will quote, with apparent approval, from the old evangelical hymn-writers, and extol the old evangelical preachers, while he and they, in many doctrinal matters, are whole hemispheres apart. On the other hand, he will interweave the opinions of advanced liberal theologians with his own in such a way as to make distinction between them very difficult, and yet protests if his readers fail to discriminate.' He gives conclusive evidence to prove that Dr Glover rejected altogether the sacrificial aspect of the atonement, and ridiculed the views of evangelicals.

Having described the Baptists, Poole-Connor turns to the Methodists of the time. He quotes from a letter to *The Times*, written from Westminster College: ' "The change from the older view of the Bible . . . took place almost without more than a few ripples on the surface of the church life. Today in all the seven English theological colleges of the Methodist churches the point of view that is known in America as fundamentalist is not represented at all . . ."

'Possessed of this perfectly frank information, the reader would be prepared to learn that the union of the three Methodist churches necessitated a very careful adaptation of their doctrinal basis to the new order of things. Dr Harold Morton, who for several years has fought strenuously for the maintenance of the conservative position, writes in an open letter to Dr Maltby as follows: "The proposed basis is so worded as to mean little or nothing . . . The sermons, the notes, the creeds, the Reformation, the Bible, all are mentioned in order that we may agree to say nothing about them. The three great churches are to unite in a theological vacuum."

'There seems little question that Dr Morton is right. The statement in the Scheme of Union that the Methodist church "loyally accepts the fundamental principles of the historic creeds and of the Protestant Reformation" sounds very reassuring, but its value as a doctrinal safeguard is practically nil. The expression "fundamental principles" means one thing to the conservative evangelical; but quite another to those who drew up the Scheme of Union. The inerrancy of Scripture, the virgin birth and infallibility of our Lord, His substitutionary atonement and bodily resurrection – these are "fundamentals" to the evangelical. But as every one of these doctrines has been denied or treated as an open question by leading Methodists, and the Wesleyan Conference has categorically refused to exercise discipline in regard to them, it is evident that they are not included in the "fundamental principles" to which loyalty is promised.'

Poole-Connor considered that the theological colleges were mainly responsible for the apostasy, being liberal in almost every case. Having proved his point he concludes as follows: 'The Reformation was mainly a return to apostolic teaching, the rediscovery of doctrines buried under human accretions. To go forward it was necessary to go back to the faith once for all delivered to the saints. Let there be such a return in our day; for in spite of the confident assertions of modern theologians, scholarship and truth are not all on one side. Let the testimony to the evangelical faith be clear and unhesitating; let it be accompanied (in God's grace) by loving compassion, spiritual power, and righteousness of life; let the lesser barriers that divide believer from believer be removed; and who can tell what may lie ahead before us?'

Thus he dealt with the terrible change that had overtaken Nonconformity. At the same time, in *The Apostasy of English Nonconformity*, he took the opportunity to introduce the Fellowship of Independent Evangelical Churches. Nearly twenty years later, in 1951, he wrote a larger work, *Evangelicalism in England*, again of an historical nature, and again advocating the Fellowship. Although he was incontestably right in his facts and prophetic in his judgements, these were uncomfortable, and therefore unwelcome. Truly he was a prophet 'without honour'.

In the same year that *Apostasy* was published, 1933, Poole-Connor was invited for the second time to the pastorate of Talbot

Tabernacle, London, at the age of sixty-one.

The 1930s is known in the political realm as the time of the 'policy of appeasement'. People wanted a quiet life, and little opposition was raised to this policy, but what there was, was usually smothered. Vested interests in the Ruhr and elsewhere were responsible for this silence, and for the suppression of the facts of German rearmament. Reporters who noted such facts were told by national dailies that their information was not wanted. A similar spirit pervaded the religious denominations. These, having lost their distinctive evangelical fervour, were now declining rapidly in membership and influence. In 1930, Dr Douglas Brown, President of the Baptist Union, spoke of the 'desperate situation' of the churches. For the religious life of England generally, the depression of the thirties was as much spiritual as it was economic. Statistics show that in spite of the rapid growth of population, church membership and Sunday Schools were falling sharply. The peak period just before World War I was followed by a steady decline that accelerated as the century progressed. It is important to note, however, that while the large denominations were shrinking, much smaller groups gained some ground. The Brethren grew a little, and Pentecostal churches sprang up. The missions of the Jeffreys brothers between 1925 and 1935 brought many people into the Pentecostal churches. It would be appropriate to state here that Poole-Connor believed that the extraordinary manifestations of the Spirit were limited, in the providence of God, to the apostolic era. He believed that they were given especially to challenge and stir the hearts of the Jews before they, as a nation, rejected the Gospel.

A unique insight into the spiritual state of the time is provided by reactions to the centenary of the birth of C. H. Spurgeon in 1934. For Poole-Connor it was a supremely important occasion. He commemorated it by organising meetings, and publishing during those celebrations an address on the 'ominous silence' concerning the

Down-Grade Controversy. Notice was given of this in the March issue of *Talbot Tabernacle Notes*: 'The majority of the readers of these *Notes* will no doubt be aware that the centenary of the birth of Charles Haddon Spurgeon is to be celebrated during the present year. For reasons that will shortly be made public, it has been decided to arrange for a series of meetings to be held independent of those officially promoted, in which the Gospel that Spurgeon preached will again be proclaimed, and the truths for which, in his protest against the departure from the evangelical faith, he so nobly stood, once more affirmed.

'These meetings, God willing, will take the form of a three-week Spurgeon Centenary Mission . . . culminating in what, it is hoped, will be a great gathering on October 8th, in the Central Hall, Westminster, at which Dr T. T. Shields and Dr Dinsdale Young will speak. So far as details can be provisionally arranged, it is thought that the first week of the mission will be allotted to Highgate Road Baptist Chapel, the second week to Lansdowne Hall, West Norwood, and the third to the Talbot Tabernacle. The main reason for the meetings being conducted in connection with these churches is that their former pastors (James Stephens, W. Fuller Gooch and Frank H. White) were closely associated with C. H. Spurgeon both before and after he left the Baptist Union; but it also happens that the buildings are conveniently situated in the north, the south and west of London respectively. The prayers of our readers are asked that in all that shall be done God may be glorified, and the souls of men benefited.'

The general committee that organised the mission issued a leaflet entitled, *What Spurgeon Taught*. It was part of Mr Spurgeon's confession of faith, and referred very directly to the inspiration of the Scriptures. Talbot Tabernacle was right behind Poole-Connor in this action, for at the end of June, while preparations were in full swing, he was invited by the church meeting to accept the 'regular' pastorate of the Tabernacle. He had been there only nine months – they did not feel it necessary to wait for the full year of customary probation.

In the August edition of the *Notes* he referred to the centenary celebrations: 'It is not often that we refer in these *Notes* to matters outside the immediate sphere of the Talbot Tabernacle; and certainly we have no desire to make their brief pages a vehicle for controversy. Nevertheless we feel that we should be coming short of our duty if we did not refer to one serious aspect of the recent Spurgeon centenary gathering. As far as we can judge from the published reports of these meetings, as well as from the reference in the current religious press, Mr Spurgeon's action in withdrawing from the Baptist Union is now regarded by the majority of Baptists as being either wholly unnecessary or actually worthy of blame; and the silence of those who must surely think otherwise permits this adverse judgement to go by default. From this criticism of Mr Spurgeon's action, and from the silence that appears to give consent to it, we desire most heartily to disassociate ourselves. The former Pastor of this church, the late beloved Frank H. White, was one of the first to range himself by the side of Mr Spurgeon when he made his great protest against error; and having heard the story from Mr White's lips, we unhesitatingly declare our conviction that, like another great Protestant, Martin Luther, Mr Spurgeon could "do no other". We grieve that those of his friends who are of this opinion do not more boldly express it.'

He gave fuller expression to this ominous silence in a published address to young people. This conveys very clearly not only Poole-Connor's attitude at this time, but the simple and forceful way he could convey these vital truths. Here is most of his address:

'Let me begin by reminding you that in order to celebrate the 100th anniversary of Mr Spurgeon's birth, a number of meetings were arranged, of which the most important were the very large gathering in the Albert Hall at which the Prime Minister presided, and the somewhat smaller ones held in the Metropolitan Tabernacle. At these meetings a number of persons, holding very varying views, joined in eulogising Mr Spurgeon and in commemorating the various aspects of his life and work.

'Now I need scarcely say that much that fell from the lips of the speakers was such as one was exceedingly thankful to hear. But there was one striking omission. No reference was made to that outstanding event of Mr Spurgeon's later life known as the Down-Grade Controversy. With one exception, scarcely to be called such, none of his old friends had anything to say about it; his grandson, Mr Harold Spurgeon, who is generally thought to hold most of his grandfather's views, made no allusion to it; and the reticence concerning it was in every way so marked that Dr Dinsdale Young said in the hearing of a friend of mine that he was tempted to call it "a conspiracy of silence".

'Quite probably you younger people did not notice this; or if you did, you attached little importance to it. Yet to some of us older men who remember Mr Spurgeon and know what the controversy meant, the careful avoidance of this subject was a matter of sincere and deep regret; and I will tell you why.

'I will begin by saying what was not the reason. It was not because it was a dead issue, a musty, fusty theme that everybody had long since forgotten, that it was avoided. On the contrary, it was such a living issue that if there had not been some agreement, tacit or otherwise, to say nothing about it, the recent celebrations would have been impossible. It was far too explosive a subject! Besides, if the question of what is the right course to pursue when leading men in one's denomination depart from the Gospel was a serious one in Mr Spurgeon's day, it is immeasurably more so today.

'Why, then, the silence? Well, first, those speakers who hold views against which Mr Spurgeon protested would naturally not mention

the matter. Secondly, those who are very strongly desirous of pre-
serving the unity of the Baptist denomination would not dwell upon
it. The late Dr Fullerton, who was quite a "sound" man himself, said
to me some years before he died, "modernism has come to stay, and
we must make the best of it." Thirdly, those who still hold Mr Spurgeon's doctrinal views, but who have come to have a great horror of
controversy, would avoid any reference to Mr Spurgeon's action, as
being both controversial in itself and provocative of controversy in
others. This attitude is now a very common one. A Baptist minister
who represents quite a large group of young evangelical ministers
said recently, at a public meeting, "We don't agree with the modernists; but we are not going to fight them," and the fact that these
silent young men have been spoken of as "Our Dumb Friends'
League" does not trouble them in the least.

'First, it seems to me to do Mr Spurgeon's memory a great injus-
tice. Not only did he suffer in his lifetime for the noble stand that
he took, but until this very moment he is being attacked on account
of it. Those who think that he was wrong are not silent, however
dumb his friends may be. Dr Reaveley Glover, for example, in the
article previously referred to, says that his leaving the Baptist Union
was due to tittle-tattle, gout, a bad conscience and the devil. For his
friends to know that these things are being said, and yet to lift no
voice in his defence in his recent memorial gatherings, seems
inexplicable.

'But, secondly, I believe this extreme dread of controversy is in
itself a dangerous thing. Controversy for its own sake I hate; but the
other extreme is equally an evil. Dr Stalker in his *Imago Christi*,
shows that to avoid it entirely is neither Christ-like nor apostolic,
and adds, "It is no good sign that controversy is looked down upon
. . . for excessive aversion to controversy may be an indication that a
church has no keen sense of possessing truth that is any great worth,
and that it has lost appreciation of the infinite difference in value

between truth and error". In the present case it means that leading evangelical Baptists have once more made up their minds not to oppose false teaching in their midst.

'Let me say here that experience shows that it is seldom possible to remain in this neutral position. It has frequently proved that the error that we refuse to oppose gradually becomes less repugnant to us. Then, too, I read the following, written by Rev F. C. Spurr, in the *British Weekly* (May, 1934): "For the first time in Baptist history, I believe, a session of the Baptist Union was held in the Metropolitan Tabernacle . . . A tribute should be paid to Rev Tydeman Chilvers, who was incarnate graciousness in welcoming the Assembly at the Tabernacle. 'Surely C. H. Spurgeon,' he said, 'must look down with pleasure upon this gathering. With all my heart I give you welcome, *welcome*, WELCOME!' To younger men," Mr Spurr continues, "this would not have meant so much as it meant to the elders, who knew the amazing significance of the welcome." It meant, of course, that Mr Spurgeon's successors have now refused to endorse his protest against error in the Union, even though that error is far more in evidence in our day than in his. *Thus, as it seems to me, Truth is built upon the one hand by orthodox preaching, and pulled down, on the other, by practical compromise.' [Italics mine, because this statement is so perceptive and relevant to the present – DGF.]*

'Finally,' continued Poole-Connor, 'I am distressed at the present policy of silence as exemplified in the centenary gatherings because it tends greatly to confuse the minds of the younger people . . . You will find that my distress is not widely shared. Indeed, many evangelical Baptists are most happy at the present condition of things. The new President of the Baptist Union, Rev Gilbert Laws, we are told, went to the recent Union meetings, at which, so to speak, the lion was lying down with the lamb and the fundamentalist and modernist feeding together, with such happiness in his heart that it kept bubbling over into song. "Happy days are come again," he was singing. I tell you, young people, apart from God's intervention, I am desperately afraid for the future. I echo Mr Spurgeon's words: "My brother thinks that we have gained a great victory. I believe that we are hopelessly sold. I feel heartbroken." But I want you to remember that there are some who have tried to keep these great issues clear; some who regard the modernist views of the Bible and of the person and work of our Lord, as so vitally wrong that not only do they honour the memory of Mr Spurgeon for his protest against them, but they feel that they cannot associate, directly or indirectly, with a Union that not only opposed and censured his action, but, when urged, refused to withdraw its censure; a Union that through its leading men, still attacks him for the stand he made. So now you know why I have spoken of the "ominous silence" at the Spurgeon centenary gatherings.'

The celebrations that Poole-Connor and others organised for the centenary exceeded their highest hopes. The spacious Talbot Tabernacle was full every night, and God honoured him for his faithful stand.

9
The Pastor and his Convictions

POOLE-CONNOR'S ministry at Talbot Tabernacle was exceptionally blessed. In his preaching he would vary his method, at times giving a series of expositions, and at others expounding individual texts, but he was always notably straightforward and direct. His children's talks continued to be a special feature. The church was a hive of activity, but all its activities were of a spiritual nature. It was not an 'institutional church' of the kind rapidly becoming popular, replete with many social activities. Tudur Jones points out that the 'conception of the church as a social centre had been growing in popularity during the last quarter of the 19th century and reached its high-water mark in the early years of the 20th. Something was found for everyone to do; no interest was left uncatered for.'[1]

'The Pleasant Sunday Afternoon movement was an indirect outcome of the Sankey and Moody Birmingham mission of 1875 . . . In many large towns crowds of a thousand and more gathered together to enjoy the mixture of orchestral music, community hymn-singing and man-to-man talking that gave to the PSA its characteristic flavour.'[2]

Describing the successful Congregationalist church of the early 20th century, Tudur Jones says, 'Any activity that was not positively irreligious was encouraged. In this way, it was hoped to keep all the members busy and enthusiastic and to attract new recruits. This conception of the nature of the Christian community was elaborated and systematised into a doctrine of the church by the protagonists of the "institutional church". Its most persuasive advocate was Charles Silvester Horne. As he expounded it, the purpose of the institutional church was to help man to develop all his faculties. Provision was made not only for the soul but for the body as well.'[3]

Tudur Jones cites as an example of the institutional church – 'Christ Church, Westminster Bridge Road, where F. B. Meyer had taken over the ministry from Newman Hall in 1892. Here a vast network of societies attracted the interest of thousands. The carefully organised PSA had an average attendance of 800. There were clubs for cricket, football, tennis, swimming, chess and draughts. There was a "Forum" where regular debates and discussions were held. There was a benevolent club, a brass band, an annual Summer Holiday Camp and a Women's At Home.'[4] Meyer was keenly interested in politics, and, though he was orthodox, he was affected by the great interest in social reform. The range of his interests broadened toward the end of his life: 'He threw himself into philanthropic and social work.'[5]

By this time the so-called 'social gospel' had, in countless churches, replaced the message of salvation: 'The kingdom of God had become an attainable social ideal. Christianity was expounded in secular terms and its traditional theological content and devotional practices contrasted unfavourably with its ethical and activist emphasis.'⁶ While Meyer was undoubtedly an orthodox evangelical, his unwise emphasis on politics and social reform was a result of this new thinking.

The activities of the Talbot Tabernacle were many, and there was something found for everyone to participate in; but these activities, as we have noted, were limited to spiritual objectives. There was, in fact, a rule at the Tabernacle that – 'Only spiritual work is carried on in the church buildings. No concerts, entertainments, or recreative meetings are held, as it is felt to be more in keeping with the divine will as revealed in the Scriptures, that they should not be undertaken by the church.' These words appear in a document entitled: 'Principle and Practice of the Talbot Tabernacle Church'. All the usual services were held on the Lord's Day, and during the week meetings provided for the different sections of the church.

Poole-Connor wrote that the Tabernacle had not swerved – 'either from its original doctrinal position or methods of service . . . both in the Tabernacle itself and in its mission hall, situated in a needy quarter, half a mile away; and it still carries on its work without resorting to entertainments or other doubtful methods of attracting visitors or securing funds. It continues, as it has ever done, to seek the salvation of the children; and God has so blessed this department of its labours that it has been able to see (as it was privileged to do at a crowded meeting of former teachers and scholars held early in the present year) one after another rising to testify to definite conversion, experienced either in earlier days or later life, as the direct result of the teachers' efforts to bring young souls to the Saviour.'

While the church had many varied activities and special meetings, the most important part of its life was undoubtedly the ministry of the Word. The regular opening up of the Word of God by their pastor was the centre of the fellowship, and the principal means of spiritual sustenance. He could not be superficial, nor would he merely produce neat but artificial divisions of the text that failed to bring out the real thought of a passage. He was truly thorough in his handling of the text, and in his presentation of it. His was, in short, 'a complete ministry – expository, doctrinal, evangelistic', a former Treasurer of the Tabernacle once stated.

In June, 1938, the jubilee of the Tabernacle was held, marking the 50th anniversary since the building was opened. The services lasted a week, and the *Bayswater Chronicle* gave great length to a report of the meetings, concluding with the comment, 'If there is one thing that the Tabernacle has stood for all the years of its existence, and still stands for, it is the full and complete inspiration of the whole Bible.' Truly, the light shone brightly at Bayswater.

Poole-Connor was deeply concerned for the many who lived around the Tabernacle, and who had no knowledge of salvation. The area was changing further, and quickly, with people of different nationalities coming in. It was becoming a mission field in the international sense. His missionary spirit was genuine, for it extended not only to the overseas field, but also to the doorstep. Open-air work, carried on for years, continued, and in January, 1939, he commenced a long series of monthly pamphlets which were circulated locally. They aimed at bringing people into the services, sometimes to hear particular people who had an interesting background.

World War II called for a deeper, spiritual explanation of terrible events for the understanding and stimulation of believers in their work for the Lord, and Poole-Connor played his part.

An illustration of Poole-Connor's faith comes out in his response to some words of Scripture pressed on his heart shortly before the Second World War. He used to pay particular attention to Scriptures which registered on his mind in the moments between sleeping and waking in the early morning. One morning the words of *Isaiah 32.18-19* had come to him: 'My people shall dwell in a peaceable habitation, and in sure dwellings, and in quiet resting places; when it shall hail, coming down on the forest.'

He had no idea what this meant at the time, but took it as a personal covenant promise. What was really involved he understood well enough later, when the rain of fire and death fell everywhere. Such a time found him living undisturbed in his flat in Bayswater, making his regular visits (as if nothing were happening) to the sick, bereaved, and wounded, and ministering the Word, as only he could, at the great Victorian Talbot Tabernacle. The Rev H. Brash Bonsall tells us, 'When through enemy action the flat became untenable, he was offered a choice of two flats in different blocks . . . The next time I saw him, serene and businesslike as always, he was seated in his study in Beaumanor Mansions . . . "If we had taken the other flat we should none of us have been here," he said. "It suffered a direct hit!"' God had still more work for him to do!

Poole-Connor was not slow to detect the alarming way some so-called Christians supported Hitler. Commenting in the FIEC *Quarterly* on Hitler's attack on Russia, he said:

'It is frequently affirmed that a clear distinction should be drawn between the German people and their Nazi rulers; the implication being that the former must not be held responsible for the action of the latter. It is devoutly to be hoped that this is the case; but there are some very disquieting symptoms. "The Lutheran Church," says the religious organ of the British Ministry of Information, "sent an effusive telegram to Hitler after the attack on Russia. The full text of the cable reads as follows: 'The Council for Spiritual Affairs of the German evangelical church, meeting for the first time since the beginning of the decisive struggle in the east, assures you, once again, our leader, in these exciting and stirring hours, of the unchangeable faithfulness and devotion of all evangelical Christians in the Reich. You, our leader, have banished the Bolshevist danger in our own country, and now call our nation and the nations of Europe to the decisive onslaught against the deadly enemy of all order and all Western Christian civilization. The German nation, and with it all its Christian members, thank you for this deed . . . It accompanies with all its prayers both you and our incomparable soldiers, who are now dealing such tremendous blows in order to clear away the plague-spot, so that a new order may arise through-out all Europe under your leadership, and an end be made of all inward dissolution, all desecration of holy things, and all offences against freedom of conscience. (Signed: D. Marahrens, Schultz D. Hymmen.)'"

'Did the writers of this letter,' Poole-Connor asked, 'lift up their protest when their Führer made a pact "to all eternity" with the Soviet? There is no available record of their making any such objec-tion. And the pact being made, with every solemnity that could constitute it a binding covenant, did the German evangelical church condone their leader's treacherous attack upon the people with whom he had just sworn everlasting friendship? It is to be assumed so. If the German church and the German people are to be judged by this document their case is not one for sympathy, but for sorrowful and compassionate prayer. They need that one teach them again what are the first principles of the oracles of God.'

Poole-Connor also gave a definite lead to those who could not see the spiritual issues of the war: 'It is a matter of no small surprise to learn that there are still some that cannot discern any clear-cut spiritual significance in the struggle now shaking the globe. To those that accept what seems to be the unequivocal teaching of Scripture – that is, that men and nations are constantly employed as the agents for carrying out the plans laid in the unseen world – it appears incredible that the titanic conflict can be no more than a meaning-less clash of merely human forces. Viewed as an effort of the evil one to cripple or crush the cause of Christ the war now raging is capable of coherent interpretation. But if it involves no moral issue; if belligerents on both sides possess equally good reason for entering upon it; if God and the devil are standing equally aloof from it; then the world is a bedlam, the historical and end-times teaching of the Bible without point or purpose, and prayer, a futility. Such as so regard public events may well cry "Alas, my Master, how shall we do?" But others, whose eyes have been opened to see the spiritual forces engaged, will rejoice to believe that the battle is not theirs, but God's, and will act and pray accordingly.'

Despite the shock and rigours of war, which should have stirred churches to self-examination, the general state of evangelicalism continued to decline. Poole-Connor commented on the state of evangelicalism in the Fellowship *Quarterly*:

'*The Record* of February 6th contained a letter from a correspondent, in which he made some disquieting statements concerning the state of evangelicalism in the Church of England . . . It was largely due, he said, to the growing worldliness of the younger evangelical clergy. "Whist drives, dances, theatricals and passion-plays," he declared, "are commonplaces now in so-called evangelical parishes." If the picture be a true one, it is not a little distressing.'

Poole-Connor's puritanism affected his day-to-day life, and his attitude towards worldliness, particularly in the house of God. In a pamphlet entitled, *Take These Things Hence,* he made a forceful protest against the introduction of theatricals, whist drives and dancing into the Christian church: 'In the Temple at Jerusalem there were certain offerings to be presented, and certain tribute-monies to be paid. For the convenience of worshippers from a distance a market was instituted in the city, where sacrifices might be purchased, and foreign currency exchanged. In process of time the market crept nearer to the Temple, until at last it obtruded itself into the sacred precincts themselves. It was against the traffic of this temple-market that our Lord lifted up His voice. Making a whip of small cords, He drove out the traders and their wares, crying "Take these things hence."

'Notice first, then, that our Lord drove out a traffic against which

He would not have protested if found elsewhere. To the market, as such, no objection was made. It was its utter incongruity with the Temple courts which roused His anger. And it is the incongruity of the theatre, the card-table, and the dancing party with the Christian church, which is the ground of our present objection. If a man making no Christian profession goes to see a decent play, or engages in a game of whist or attends a ball, we have nothing to say against it. Such things are the amusements of the world, and the world will have its own. It is useless to expect a man to separate himself from that of which he is part and parcel. But when these things are brought into the Christian church, the case is wholly different. There is no compatibility between this traffic of the world and the house of God, and its presence is an intrusion and an outrage. "Take these things hence." We do not object to them because they are necessarily immoral or dishonest, but because, in the essence of things, they are utterly out of place.

'For consider what the Temple was. It was a sacred edifice. It was – in purpose at least – the dwelling-place of the Most High. It was the place where, in type, the great truths of atonement and divine mercy were proclaimed. It was the place where the publican crying "God be merciful to me a sinner" could find grace, and go down to his house justified. It was the place of common praise and prayer and exposition of the sacred Word – what right, amid all these high and holy things, had the dust and noise of the market? But the church, too, has been "builded together for an habitation of God through the Spirit". It is a sacred institution, through which God may meet the highest and the deepest needs of men. To bring into its courts – even its outer courts – the farce, the card-table, the polka and the waltz, is a desecration and an offence. And if (as is so often done) the plea of necessity is raised, the answer is clear. With far greater reason might the Temple traders have raised the plea of necessity for their traffic; yet the Lord drove them out, for all that.

'But let us guard against a misunderstanding. Our meaning is not for one moment that provided these things are not brought into the church, the Christian is free to seek them elsewhere. If the theatre, the card-table, and the dance, are out of place in the Christian church, they are no less out of place in the Christian life. For the Christian, too, is the temple of God. He is bidden to present his body as "a living sacrifice, holy, acceptable unto God". He is the sacred instrument of the divine will. Within the sphere of his life, no less than within the Temple courts, the things that are of the world, worldly, are equally an intrusion and an incongruity. From them both our Lord would drive them out.

'If it be objected that this is a narrow and an unacceptable view, then we must fall back on a direct scriptural command – "Be not conformed to this world." Does anyone pretend that if a Christian is watching a theatrical piece, or a music-hall turn, or playing a game of cards, or joining in a dance, he is not being conformed to this world? What else is he doing? Nor can we admit the plea that if this prohibition be so interpreted it would equally forbid all innocent physical and mental recreation – would shut out a game of golf or a game of chess – seeing that the world also engages in these things. Not so. The "world" eats and drinks, sleeps and walks, but these things are not therefore "worldly". There are many neutral things which belong to man as man, and innocent recreation is one of them. But the theatre, the card-parties, and the ball are peculiarly and specially things of the world. The mark of the world is unmistakable upon them. Who except those who want an excuse would ever question it? Let us be honest. Let us either say frankly that we no longer accept the New Testament teaching concerning nonconformity to the world; or else, accepting it, let us admit that theatre-going, card-playing and dancing are wholly incompatible with the Christian profession. "TAKE THESE THINGS HENCE."'

In 1941, in addition to the removal of many families from central

London, two Tabernacle elders died who were very generous men, and contributed greatly to the Lord's work. The Tabernacle went through a difficult period financially, and Poole-Connor, in spite of the fact that he had no private income, returned a part of his salary. He sent out a letter to members of the congregation, in which he told them of the position of the church as to its resources and its needs. The war had not only scattered the flock, but laid increased burdens upon those who remained.

The large Sunday Schools at the Tabernacle and the mission hall had 'vanished in a day, on the declaration of war', through child evacuation, as we learn from the *Tabernacle Notes* of June-July, 1942, 'but the teachers have again set themselves, with the utmost seriousness, to solve the problem which the pagan child-life of the district presents; and in so doing they deserve (and, we are sure, receive) the sympathy and prayer-support of our congregation. They realise – what is, indeed, patent to all – that while the old evangelical truths are still firmly to be held and taught, new methods of approach must be found; and they have evolved a scheme for securing and maintaining the attendance of young people which we believe to be a sound and wise one. Those concerned for the welfare of youth today are faced by a twofold danger; that of adopting, on the one hand, schemes that are so tinged with worldliness as to be contrary to the plain teaching of Scripture; and, on the other, that of clinging to non-essential methods of work that are obviously obsolete. It is our belief that our teachers have been so guided of God as to escape both dangers; and already there are signs that their efforts will be rewarded with the divine blessing.'

Late in 1943, Poole-Connor gave formal intimation of his resignation from the Tabernacle. His second pastorate had lasted ten years, and he was now seventy-one years old. He wrote: 'A new prospect is, I believe, opening up before the church. The worst of the raids on London (at least, on any continuous scale) are, I trust, over. I have been with you through some dark days. I have sorrowed with you in your bereavements. I have stood by while members of our church have been dug out of their bombed dwellings. I have buried your dead. I have seen our two fine Sunday Schools vanish in a night. Now the tide is turning. Young life is beginning to flow back. The number of those attending our Sunday Schools is rapidly growing. A new personality, a new voice, new energy, new (though scriptural) methods, are now called for and these two concurrent considerations are to me a clear indication as to the choice God would have me make.

'There is no need for any formal "goodbye". We are not moving far out of London, although we are quitting our present dwelling, and on any occasion when you want me, and I am free, I can come in and see you. For the same reason no elaborate thanks are necessary. All I need say is, for much kindness received, God bless you; and as to your future, God guide you.'

The Church Secretary duly replied: 'During the time you have been with us there have been many tokens of God's blessing and favour and I, personally, cannot think of the Tabernacle without you. I do, however, realise that you feel torn in two directions as God is undoubtedly blessing your testimony far beyond the confines of the Tabernacle, and if you feel the step you contemplate is of the Lord, I for one, can but pray that our great loss may be somebody else's gain. When the apostle left the believers long ago they sorrowed that they would see his face no more. If it is in the providence of God that you should leave us, we too shall sorrow, but we shall still hope sometimes to see your face and even hear your voice.'

Thus the pilot had steered the ship through two difficult periods. His task now at the age of seventy-one was to be a watchman and guide for confused evangelicals at large, in an increasingly complex age. This he was to do for another eighteen years.

Notes

1   R. Tudur Jones, *Congregationalism in England 1662-1962*, Independent Press, p. 315.
2   Tudur Jones, ibid., p 317.
3   Tudur Jones, ibid., p 318.
4   Tudur Jones, ibid., p 319.
5   A. C. Underwood, *A History of the English Baptists*, Carey Kingsgate, London, 1947.
6   Tudur Jones, ibid., p. 343.

10

Wielding the Pen of Faith

MOST MEN have retired by the time they reach their seventies, but Poole-Connor, at the age of seventy-one, still had a long period of intense activity before him. It was indeed for him, as someone said, a 'glorious sunset'. Like Caleb, he used his enduring strength for further exploits, and gave repeated expression to the clear convictions God had given him, at a time when many Christians were confused and society was adrift.

His spiritual interests were many, but he was chiefly concerned with the Fellowship of churches he had been the means of founding. The Council of the Fellowship of Independent Evangelical Churches coined for him the title 'National Commissioner'. It was a unique title for one whose services were unique. He travelled the length and breadth of the land visiting many churches, as he had done years previously in the service of the North Africa Mission, but this time he focused on churches that were bound together in fellowship, and how those churches welcomed him! In every way he was equipped to be an elder statesman: always definite in his interpretation of Scripture, yet courteous to the views of others. A voracious reader, he kept himself abreast with current spiritual affairs and trends of thought. He could always be relied on as a logical thinker, and he expressed himself clearly as one brought up to have deep admiration for the English language. His library contained numerous choice volumes of English literature, and it was always a pleasure to listen to his diction. He was never above speaking to small companies of the Lord's people, but gave himself to the work, whether it meant addressing a thousand in central London, or a dozen in a village mission hall. Until his illness, shortly before his death, he preached nearly every Sunday, besides mid-week engagements, for the Lord spared him his faculties wonderfully right until the end.

In 1942 he had issued the book *Evangelical Unity*, tracing the need for, and best approach to, fellowship among true Bible churches. Now, in 1943, he produced a most significant booklet entitled *Denominational Confusion and the Way Out*. In this, Poole-Connor begins by demonstrating the essential unity that existed between the larger Protestant bodies on the essentials of the faith, until the advent of higher criticism in the 19th century. The points of difference between them lay only in matters of church government and ordinances. However, he shows that since the advent of higher criticism, and then modernism, this unity had completely gone: 'The Free Churches of today would as little think of subscribing to the Westminster Confession, or to the original doctrinal basis of the Evangelical Alliance, as they would of pledging themselves to the theory of a flat earth. Beyond their strictly sectarian significance, denominational names now convey nothing. To be introduced to a person as being a Presbyterian, or a Congregationalist, or a Baptist, or a Methodist, affords no clue whatever to his really essential beliefs. It does not even indicate whether he is an out-and-out Protestant, or is on his way towards Rome.'

He points out further that if a Baptist wanted to baptise infants, or a Congregationalist wished to repudiate Congregational government, they would be obliged to leave their respective denominations, whereas on almost every other doctrinal topic they would have freedom to remain. 'If they alter their views on questions of governing or being governed in their churches, or of using much water or little water at their baptismal services, naturally they must go; these are things that really count. But where it is a mere matter of the seat of authority in religion, or the reliability of our Lord's utterances, or the nature of the atonement, or whether conversion is to be psychologically or supernaturally explained – in other words, where it is a question of doctrines which used to be regarded as vital – why leave? On these points everyone now is free to believe what he likes.'

Poole-Connor shows this to be confusion of the worst kind, especially amongst Nonconformists, many of whom regard baptism as a 'fundamental', and the evangelical faith as a 'non-essential'. He suggests a 'way out'. (We remember that he is not counselling churches to abandon their distinctive beliefs in church government and the ordinances, but only to regard them as being no bar to cordial fellowship between congregations.)

He writes: 'Let the bond of union henceforth be the great verities of the evangelical faith, and let the liberty of individual conviction be in regard to the lesser issues. The principle is already operating successfully – has been, indeed, for over twenty-one years – in the movement referred to, the Fellowship of Independent Evangelical Churches. In this spiritual brotherhood, churches, missions, ministers, evangelists, and Christian workers generally, unite, first on the ground of a common experience of the saving power of the Lord Jesus Christ, and then on the basis of a common belief in the evangelical faith, rightly and historically interpreted. (There are many that claim the title of evangelical who have no just right to it.)

While not departing from their individual convictions as to church administration, they believe that the preservation of the evangelical faith must be their chief concern. With this as the common denominator they find it possible to co-operate in the utmost cordiality of spirit with those who differ from them in lesser matters.'

We have observed already that this desirable formula for unity would eventually be severely strained and less workable, with the arrival of post-1960 trends in the churches.

Poole-Connor possessed an outstanding intellect, and during this latter period of his life he not only defended the faith in a scholarly way, but encouraged others to deepen their knowledge and methods of study. At the end of World War II he took a leading part in the resurrection of All Nations Bible College. Just before the war the building had been sold, the money put into the bank, and the furniture into storage. Through Poole-Connor the College's ruling council was re-convened, and the College restarted in part of the premises of Kensit College, Finchley. He became the first post-war Principal, holding this post for three years. It required no little faith to undertake such a venture. For the first term he and his three helpers, together with his wife, worked for the one solitary student. That student later became the Principal of a Bible College. The Rev H. Brash Bonsall, who helped Poole-Connor at this time, recalls: 'At dinner on one occasion, as we all sat clustered round this poor student, I said, "I wonder, Mr Poole-Connor, where we shall all be in three years' time?" Little did we realise that within that time the College, by the good hand of God upon it, should have thirty-seven students, housed in various buildings, including a forty-four roomed, two centuries old mansion, set in seven acres of beautiful grounds.'

Among other subjects Poole-Connor taught church history and Old Testament studies. Through the organ of the *College Review* he made his statesmanlike comments on the times. In the spring issue of 1947 he wrote an article entitled, 'The Hour, the Need and the Remedy', in which he summed up the world situation masterfully. He foresaw such events as the rise of Russia as a hostile power, the restrictions on the Gospel in India, and the increasing strength of Rome. He held to the conviction that God would yet intervene as He had done so frequently in the past. In spite of the darkness there were some signs of encouragement. He referred to the recent flow of candidates for the mission field, and mentioned that it was in antici-pation of just such a movement that the College had been reopened. Its curriculum had been drawn up mainly, though not exclusively, for those called to the foreign field.

He was an excellent Principal and was easy to work with. He was never too hurried to be a good listener, and was always ready to hear the views of younger men. He was still amazingly fit and well at seventy-five, and it was noted that he was capable of running half a mile to catch a train without seeming to show any concern. In July, 1948, he retired as Principal to become Principal Emeritus, but this was no office of honour only, without duties. Every week he trav-elled down to the College, now at Taplow, from his London home to give three hours of lectures. Such activities were maintained alongside his involvement in other evangelical societies, such as the Lord's Day Observance Society, of which he was Chairman from 1944.

His greatest literary work, *Evangelicalism in England*, was pub-lished when he was seventy-nine (1951). A remarkable volume in every way, it reveals a mind that has not only been saturated with church history, but also English literature. The style is charming and yet powerful, very similar to that of the great historian, Lord Macaulay. Acclaimed as an accurate and compelling survey of spir-itual blessing, its conclusions were not well received by some. A reviewer in *The Christian*, a widely circulated interdenominational monthly newspaper at the time, began by commending the work, but then spent most of his columns heavily qualifying the commendation. To him Poole-Connor was pessimistic in his assessment of the evangelical situation. The reviewer could not agree with his statement that, 'In most Protestant denominations some evangelicals are found, but they are in a minority.' The reviewer said, 'We feel that he would be as astonished as Elijah was in his day to discover how many there are who have not bowed the knee to Baal. At no time have evangelicals been so numerous in the world as they are today.'

Poole-Connor's letter of response was characteristically incisive and humorous: 'I am still somewhat puzzled as to your reviewer's estimate of the relative strength of evangelicals in this country. He seems to adhere to the comparison of them to the "remnant according to the election of grace" in apostate Israel; on the other hand he appears to imply that they are 7,000 more numerous than I imagine them to be. Can I really be so far out?'

The Principal of the London Bible College, Dr E. F. Kevan, on the other hand, writing in another popular evangelical newspaper, *Life of Faith*, gave the book a warm reception, saying, 'I would like to see it read by every theological student, every minister, and every thoughtful Christian man and woman. It is historical in its approach, but is written to plead a cause. It is delightful to read an argument – for it is an argument – so clearly and forcefully presented.' He commended Poole-Connor for his definition of the word 'evangelical': 'The real battle today is with the fifth-columnist, who wears our own uniform, but is in the camp of the enemy. In other words, the great terms which for centuries have served to enshrine the great and precious truths of the Gospel are now used to represent alien ideas. There is scarcely a word of the Gospel vocabulary which has not been stolen away in this manner.'

A passage of the greatest importance occurs in *Evangelicalism in England* (pages 283-284) which precisely and graphically defines

Poole-Connor's mature view of the need, not only for evangelical unity, but for active separation from doctrinally unsound denominations:

'If all who have not departed from the doctrine of Christ – all who in particular hold fast to Holy Scripture as the authoritative, the inerrant, the veritable, Word of God – determine that they will no longer encourage *[by remaining in the same denomination]* those who would unbar the door to Rome, or break down the wall that separates the evangelical faith from modernistic denials of it, a great testimony might yet be borne. But let it be emphatically repeated – *words are not enough*. It is action that is demanded. The lesson is so placarded that all that run may read it. Evangelicals who remain in complacent fellowship with those that deny their faith are not only failing to stem the tide of apostasy; they are accelerating its pace.

'Their very leniency is eloquent advocacy; it cries aloud to multitudes that what men call liberalism in religion is far from being the harmful thing that Spurgeon thought it, for are not they – outstanding evangelicals – hand-in-glove with those who teach it? That the ebb-tide now runs like a mill-race is due, more than to aught else, to this damaging quiescence. As in the earlier history of Israel, there was a time of crisis when by their watercourses evangelicals had great searchings of heart; but, as then, the peaceful pipings of the sheep-folds made a greater appeal than the trumpet-tones of war. Reuben remained with his flocks; Gilead and Dan and Asher abode by their creeks; Meroz came not to the help of the Lord against the mighty.

'Today further silken fetters are being woven for their feet. The voice of ridicule is dying away. The rough Reaveley Glover method of dealing with orthodoxy has given place to a sympathetic and even flattering approach. Those who were once mocked are now told that every point of view has its contribution to make to the sum-total of truth; that there is no conceivable reason why evangelical and

modernist – nay, why Protestant and Romanist – should not come together in brotherly concord. "Errors are much more likely to be overcome by discussion round the fireside in a home than by slogans shouted at one another across the street," more than one apparently friendly adviser assures them. "The simile requires, of course," the persuasive voice continues, "that the door should be opened, and an invitation be given to that fireside discussion. The door has often been tightly closed; it was opened at Amsterdam."*
With the sun thus kindly shining upon him, the evangelical traveller is far more likely to drop his cloak than when the boisterous wind sought to wrest it from him by force.

'But let not those who love the ancient faith be misled. If more than half a century ago Spurgeon had occasion to write, "It now becomes a serious question how far those who abide by the Truth once delivered to the saints should fraternise with those who have turned to another gospel," how much more urgent is the question today! And how much more insistent is the call for united evangelical action! Lesser points of difference need to be given a subordinate place in face of a common peril; the distinction between that which is vital and that which is incidental requires to be newly assessed, and substance to be given to the vision which Spurgeon's death prevented his realising.'

In the midst of this stirring passage occur the words, 'that the ebb-tide now runs like a mill-race is due, *more than to aught else,* to this damaging quiescence' *[italics ours].* He saw that the compromise of men of God had brought us to the appalling condition in which we find ourselves. Since he wrote *Evangelicalism in England,* his convictions have been acknowledged and approved of by many more than those who received them in 1951. The critical reviewer in *The*

---

*The World Council of Churches' inaugural assembly, Amsterdam, August 1948.

Christian had said, 'Often it is only when we view events in the per-spective of history that we can perceive the extent to which God was at work. Our fathers builded better than they knew, and it may be the same with our generation.' Time has proved, however, that Poole-Connor was not a pessimist but a realist.

In the same year as this volume appeared, a secular work entitled, *English Life and Leisure,* was published (Longmans, 1951), which gave a thorough survey of the behaviour of English society. This included alarming figures concerning the changed habits and falling church attendance that had taken place over the previous fifty years. Total church attendance was about a third of what it had been in 1901. The Anglicans had lost most heavily, but the Nonconformists, though consequently more numerous than the Anglicans, had a larger proportion of older people. Sunday Schools also had decreased greatly since the beginning of the century. Attendance had declined from five and a half million to one million, while the population had gone up by about a third. (Since 1951 the decline has continued even more steeply.)

In the July of the year following *Evangelicalism in England* Poole-Connor celebrated his eightieth birthday, visiting the United States and Canada, where he had many opportunities of speaking with like-minded men of God, preaching and broadcasting.

Another year on and this faithful contender made a momentous personal statement about the (British) Evangelical Alliance. In view of the fact that he had supported it for many years, and because he was a man who never hastily arrived at a decision, his resignation from the Alliance showed that, for him, unity among evangelicals must involve separation from compromise. He wrote (in the *Quarterly Record* of the FIEC):

'I am asking the Editor's permission to make a brief statement concerning my recent resignation from the Evangelical Alliance. My only purpose in so doing is to call attention to the vague and indefinite policy in regard to the World Council of Churches *[a deeply compromised body]* which the Alliance has evidently decided to pursue. One cannot but regret the difference in its present spirit from that which animated it when it gave such whole-hearted support to Charles Haddon Spurgeon in his protest against the inroads of error. When that "Valiant for Truth" left the Baptist Union . . . the Evangelical Alliance was the first to stand by his side.

'Its attitude to the World Council *[the Evangelical Alliance stated]* was to be one of "benevolent neutrality". On learning this I wrote a letter to *The Christian* newspaper, mildly expressing my regret. To my surprise the Editor refused it admission to his columns. I then inquired of the Editor of the *English Churchman* whether he would print it, and he cordially agreed to do so. But once more my efforts were frustrated, for the Bishop of Barking (Honorary Clerical Secretary of the Alliance) intervened, with neither apology nor explanation, to prevent its publication.

'Friends of the Alliance, however, bade me be patient; told me that efforts were being made to secure a less ambiguous policy; but when the statement of it at length appeared it amounted to very little more than that which had been originally issued. Finally, in the May number of *Evangelical Christendom* *[organ of the Alliance]* for the present year *[1952]* an article appeared which (however unintentionally) conveyed the impression that the World Council was strongly swinging over to evangelicalism. It dwelt with laudable satisfaction upon the efforts of certain of its more conservatively-minded members to introduce an evangelical reference to the second advent into the programme of its next congress; but it wholly omitted to mention that the attempt was categorically and even violently opposed by the modernists within its ranks.

'That no editorial or other effort was made to present the case in its true perspective, appeared to me to be "benevolent partiality" of the most marked kind. I could see that the Alliance had made up its mind to follow a policy of "benevolence" toward the World Council which carries it far beyond "neutrality", and that I was compromising my own testimony by remaining one of its members. I therefore withdrew from formal association with it, giving as my reasons the matters outlined above. E. J. Poole-Connor.'

In 1952 Poole-Connor joined with others in the formation of the British Evangelical Council,* linking groups of churches such as the FIEC that stood against false ecumenism. This Council took a similar stance at national level to that of the ICCC (the International Council of Christian Churches) at the international level. This latter body actively opposed the World Council of Churches but, as T. H. Bendor-Samuel wrote, 'The [FIEC] Council fully shared its opposition to the ecumenical movement but not the belligerent spirit of the ICCC's meetings and publications, and declined an invitation to join the movement.' He added, 'Mr Poole-Connor accepted the Council's decision but so strongly supported the ICCC's defence of the faith that he maintained his personal membership of a committee that was set up in this country to further its aims.'[1] Poole-Connor also served on the governing Council of the ICCC. He understood the objections people had to the ICCC, but also felt keenly the need for a very firm opposition to the WCC. (He expressed these views on one occasion to the author.)

The ICCC clearly maintained what has been described as 'second-degree separation', that is, separation from evangelical brethren who are themselves actively compromised. It was the style rather than the substance of the ICCC that put off the FIEC Council. It is also clear

---

*In its earliest days the British Evangelical Council linked the FIEC with such groups as the Free Church of Scotland and the Free Presbyterian Church of Northern Ireland. It held an inspirational annual conference and a residential study conference, and generally promoted the anti-ecumenical cause. It developed its activities in subsequent years, and more recently has changed its name and widened its objectives.

from T. H. Bendor-Samuel's book that in practice the FIEC did follow second-degree separation in the early days. Dr Martyn Lloyd-Jones, in his *Maintaining the Evangelical Faith Today*, took the very same position. He objected to the style of the ICCC but not its position. He also held to second-degree separation.

The founder of the ICCC was Dr Carl Macintyre, an American Bible Presbyterian of immense energy. Poole-Connor recounted to the author that he had told his brethren on the FIEC Council: 'Dr Macintyre is our greatest asset and our greatest liability.' Subsequent events vindicated his misgivings, and many who had stood with Dr Macintyre withdrew from the ICCC.

In the autumn of 1954 Poole-Connor was invited to become Editor of the *Bible League Quarterly*, a journal which would subsequently carry very many editorials of the most illuminating and searching kind examining the ongoing decline of evangelicalism. He had previously contributed articles such as those critiquing the World Council of Churches, and the *Revised Standard Version*, and a notable feature – 'Authority in Religion'. Furthermore, he was a Vice-President of the Bible League, which stood unequivocally for the verbal inerrancy of the Word of God. The *Quarterly* provided scholarly answers to the higher critics together with warnings against compromise. Bishop D. A. Thompson of the Independent Church of England (a secession group) was given the task of persuading him to accept the post. 'I can almost see the light in his face now,' he remarked. 'I think he was gratified to be asked if he would help us in this way.'

This task necessarily brought Poole-Connor into further controversy, but he conducted it in a most gentlemanly and Christian way. Thus, at the age of eighty-three, he undertook this new work, and carried it on brilliantly until the illness which overtook him in the autumn of 1961, shortly before his death. The council of the Bible League pointed out that in the most difficult field of controversy, 'he was irreproachable, never lacking either in courage or in courtesy'.

He made plain his policy as Editor in his first editorial: 'It is the business of the council of the Bible League to direct the policy of its magazine; but as far as I am able to interpret it, its purpose is to confirm the faith of Christian believers in Holy Scripture – a faith inwrought and developed by the Holy Spirit, but often assailed by current unbelief – to bring godly scholarship to bear upon the questions which the doctrine of biblical authority naturally raises . . .

'I believe that it is also the council's wish that warning should be given, as need arises, of the dangers which threaten these Christian doctrines, and that erroneous teaching concerning them should be courteously but firmly rebutted. In the task of seeking such articles for the magazines as will best serve these ends, we shall be grateful for our readers' prayers.'

He addressed himself to his task immediately, and in the same issue dealt with the confusion on the sponsoring committee of the Billy Graham campaign in Scotland. Quoting from the *Monthly Record* of the Free Church of Scotland, he pointed out that a certain Dr Gunn had described fundamentalism as false, and yet had been put on the committee that supervised the campaign.

Poole-Connor's firmness was a strange spectacle to an increasing number of people. Could things really be so bad? Was it our duty to speak out against error? Was this not simply being negative? Surely, people argued, we must get on with evangelism, and not worry so much about doctrine. Poole-Connor was, however, a true pastor, and was anxious to preserve the spiritual diet of young and inexperienced Christians, lest one or two drops of poison should ruin their health. He could see better than most which truths were vitally related to the Gospel, and which were of secondary importance. As Editor of the *Quarterly*, he contended earnestly for the faith. He saw that any teaching that undermined the Gospel itself should be treated in the same way as the apostle Paul treated the Galatian heresy. He did not shrink from the task of exposing subtle deflections from biblical doctrine, even when these were expounded by famous evangelical teachers, or influential Christian periodicals.

His attitude towards Billy Graham and the crusade in Scotland at this time is evident from his comments in the spring and summer issues of the *Quarterly* (1955): 'Dr Graham's evangelistic campaign in Scotland seems to have exceeded all expectations, both in numbers attending and in professed conversions. We are thankful that he continues to make the authority of Scripture the basis of his preaching. Speaking purely for ourselves, we believe him to be a man raised up of God to preach the Gospel to the multitudes. We judge him to be sound in all the fundamentals of the Christian faith; and we have had personal contact with those who have given every evidence of having passed from death unto life under his ministry, but it would be idle, we think, to attempt to justify every feature of the campaign as a whole.

'For example, Dr William C. Somerville writes thus in *The Christian* of May 13th: "Another characteristic of the crusade in Scotland has been co-operation. Presbyterians have worked with Baptists, and Anglicans with Brethren. People holding different views on the precise way in which the Bible is God's inspired Book have worked together, too; liberals with conservatives, conservatives with liberals, and both with the liberal-conservatives, of whom there are very large numbers in Scotland . . . When each person was humble enough to acknowledge that he might not fully understand all the answers and that there might be something of great value in the views held by others, amazing things happened . . . I trust that the eight denominations so far committed to 'Tell Scotland' will keep the door open . . . and that everything will be done to avoid, or if necessary to rectify, any appearance of disunity between different members of God's family working in His name."

'Surely there is great confusion here. We are all for interdenominational co-operation where there is underlying unity in the basic Christian doctrines; but joint-action between Bible-believers and Bible-doubters; between those whose views on the person and work of our Lord are poles asunder – for all this may be included in the terms "conservative" and "liberal" – is to us incomprehensible. What common authority can they acknowledge? What common Gospel can they preach? Nor should we be led astray by the pseudo-humility which bids us admit that we do not "understand all the answers". So far as the fundamentals of the faith are concerned, we *do,* by grace, understand all the answers; for Christ and the Scriptures have taught us what they are. The lesson surely is that while we may be convinced that a movement may be, in the main, a work of God, we are under no obligation to accept all that accompanies it as being equally within His will.'[2]

The *Bible League Quarterly* gave opportunity for Christians to write for advice, or give important information concerning trends. The 'new evangelicalism', with its change of strategy from one of separation from circles where error prevailed, to that of infiltration into their ranks, was beginning to show itself in the USA, and the *Quarterly* was quick to sense it. It was, of course, already in Britain, as these pages have shown.

Poole-Connor's penetrating insight into harmful tendencies is well illustrated in his review of Berkouwer's, *Triumph of Grace in Karl Barth*: 'Dr Berkouwer's recent volume has been very favourably reviewed in most *[evangelical]* Christian periodicals. It is praised for its fairness, its comprehensive presentation of the Barthian theology, and its frank criticism of such features of the latter as the author regards as untenable. We are indebted to such theologians as Professor Berkouwer for summarising his teaching, and drawing attention to its more salient points.'

After dealing generally with the book, he makes this shrewd

comment: 'The truth is – and it is evident throughout the whole of this most massive work – that the learned and accomplished author is so frequently anxious to find a way of escape for his – shall we say client? – as often greatly to minimise the danger of his teaching. All who put themselves to the labour of reading this book should carefully bear this in mind.' At that time so very few in England were reviewing theological books with real perception, and with a readiness to identify compromise with modernism. As a reviewer, Poole-Connor was again a true contender for the faith, always uniting clarity with courtesy, but giving his readers the necessary warnings of disloyalty to the Word.

Notes

1 T. H. Bendor-Samuel, *Keeping the Faith*, p. 46.
2 The All-Scotland Crusade attracted large numbers of people. Tom Allen published a book shortly after the crusade giving facts and figures of the results of the mission. However, a very detailed survey of the effects over a longer period did not tell the same story by any means. (John Highet, *The Scottish Churches*, Skeffington & Son, London, 1960, Ch. 4, 'To What End? An Appraisal of Effect,'.)

11

Responding to Issues

A NOTABLE HIGH point for the promotion of the ecumenical movement came in 1957 when a major united gathering
of missionary societies (chiefly evangelical) was convened
to press all kinds of Christians to work together. The keynote message was preached by a well-known 'evangelical', Bishop Stephen
Neill. Poole-Connor's appraisal of these proceedings is typical of his
brilliance in description and analysis. In the *Bible League Quarterly*
of summer 1957, he wrote:

'At the opening meeting of the London Missionary Convention,
held in the Central Hall, Westminster, on March the 4th last, repre-
senting some sixty British missionary societies, an impressive – one
might almost say massive – speech was delivered by Bishop Stephen
Neill. The Bishop describes himself as a working missionary, and his
diocese, we believe, is that of Tinnevelli, in South India; but he is
also very prominent as a strong advocate of the modern ecumenical
movement; the movement, that is, for the present co-operation of

all the churches of Christendom, and their ultimate reunion . . .

'The picture of the forces massing against the Christian faith was conveyed in such a manner as to make a great impact upon the closely attentive audience; and by the time this stage of the Bishop's address was reached everyone was thoroughly prepared for what was to follow – the majority, we should judge, was indeed ready to welcome and assent to it. It was, of course, this; the church must re-model her strategy: she was, in fact, already doing so: those engaged in world-wide presentation of the Gospel must unite as varied sections of one army. The remedy was as simple as that.

'It was all very skilfully done. The need for a union of Christian effort was not so much argued as shown to be inevitable, forced on us by the irresistible logic of facts. There is nothing elaborate about the method that the Bishop and others adopt. A clear, powerful review of the forces arrayed against Christianity is presented; the terms in which it is stated are unexceptionable; and it is based on facts which none can deny. Very well; what are we all going to do about it? Is anyone going to be foolish enough as to suggest that we ought *not* to get together? Look how the magnificent unity of the Church of Rome rebukes us – Bishop Neill did not hesitate to say this in plain terms – while we Protestants are all in "rags and tatters". Thus the large audience sat, a considerable part of it consisting of evangelicals, all being gently bludgeoned in the most deft and charming manner possible, with scarcely a word that jarred, into the belief that not to commit the whole missionary effort to the ecumenical principle – the principle of world-wide co-operation in preaching Christ on a world-wide scale – was simply foolishly unthinkable.

'The Chairman, the Rev George B. Duncan, anticipated the verdict of the jury before the distinguished counsel began his speech: "We simply *have* to get together," he said: "after all, we are preaching the same Gospel." We confess we almost caught our breath at the latter remark; it seemed so curiously naive and remote from actuality. We could not but wonder, for example, if we were all preaching the same Gospel, why the Bible Churchmen's Missionary Society should have found it necessary to break away from the Church Missionary Society. *[The former was formed as a reaction to the increasing control of Anglo-Catholics in the latter.]*

'But let us examine the matter a little more closely . . . What, in plain fact, does this "getting together" mean? We cannot do better than turn to Bishop Neill himself for an answer. It is set forth, with his usual mastery of phrasing, in chapter six of the volume entitled, *The Coming of Age of Christianity.*

'We believe Bishop Neill to be wholly mistaken, but wholly sincere; the more dangerous a guide for that very reason. The pilot who is so certain that he is making for the harbour entrance that he drives full speed ahead in a fog will, if he be mistaken, pile up his vessel in the breakwater, a total and hopeless wreck; while the more cautious will escape damage. Nevertheless, obvious sincerity claims recognition and courtesy.

'First, then, in his chapter on "The Union of the Churches", Bishop Neill does not hesitate to advocate co-operation with the Church of Rome, for which he has the greatest possible admiration. "The Roman Catholic Church," he says, "is both the largest and the greatest of Christian bodies, and has preserved in their purest form some indispensable Christian values. More than any other it has laid stress upon visible unity as a necessary character of the body of Christ on earth. It is true that the particular form in which the Church of Rome has insisted on that unity has been, more than any other factor, the cause of permanent divisions within that body; but the unwavering insistence on unity presents itself as a challenge to all the separated parts. The grand Roman discipline is unlike anything found elsewhere in Christendom."

'It is difficult not to rub one's eyes. Is the dreadful story of the means by which Rome has maintained her solidarity: the rack, the stake, the inquisition, the Huguenot and Piedmontese massacres – a persecution never repented of, and still maintained in spirit – to be gently dismissed as the "particular form in which the Church of Rome has insisted on unity"? If that is so, it is indeed one of God's greatest mercies that "the grand Roman discipline is unlike anything else found in Christendom." What, too, are the indispensable doctrines and practices "preserved in their purest form" in the Roman Church, which are not found elsewhere? Are they the doctrine of justification by works, or the worship of the virgin, or the sacrifice of the mass? But we must not be drawn aside. Our present purpose is to point out that, in all earnestness and steadfastness of thought, as we believe, Bishop Neill's advocacy of Christian unity on the mission field, as in other spheres, includes co-operation with Rome, *as she is*. Protestants must give up their "intransigence", as he terms it, and labour with her, unchanged though she be in character and doctrine; for are not we "all preaching the same Gospel"? Certainly the Bishop believes it to be so. "More than any other church," he says, "Rome has kept before it as an obligation the preaching of the Gospel throughout the world. At a time when Protestants were wasting all their strength in endless sectarian quarrels, the missionaries and martyrs of the Roman obedience were laying down their bones on the shores of almost every one of the seven seas."

'It may easily be believed that after thus having been counselled to swallow the camel, the gnats of lesser divisions in doctrine are not greatly to be regarded. In a lengthy argument, couched in the pleasantest of terms, Bishop Neill shows how – in his view – every form of professed Christianity, from Romanism to Quakerism, has its contribution to make to the grand total of the Christian faith. Nor does he desire that the differences in outlook should be disguised. "If it can be made clear to the churches which at present hold aloof," he says, "that the special values for which they stand will not be jeopardised by closer co-operation with Christians of other allegiances, there is hope that they may gradually find their place within the developing world-wide movement of the churches." Truth and error, in other words, have vanished as such; mutually exclusive doctrines are merely matters of "other allegiances"; no "values", for which people have even died, are jeopardised by union with those who teach the exact opposite; whatever we believe, we are "all preaching the same Gospel".

'Finally – and here we touch the testimony to which the Bible League is dedicated – "getting together", as advocated by Bishop Neill, means co-operation with those who no longer accept the Bible as the authoritative and inerrant Word of God. Is there anyone so ill-informed, at this late hour of the day, as not to be aware of the ravages of destructive criticism on the mission field? It is the present fashion to ignore it; Bishop Neill's reference to the subject in the volume quoted is the ultimate form of vagueness. Yet the matter is nothing short of vital. What *is* the Gospel that we are all supposed to be preaching? Where is authority for the Christian faith to be found? "In the Scriptures, plus tradition and papal decrees", replies the Romanist. "In the verifying inward light", says the modernist. "In such parts of an otherwise fallible Bible as appeal to the reader with the force of inspiration", declares the Barthian. Not so was it with our Lord. "Then opened he their understanding, that they might understand the scriptures, and said unto them, thus it is written . . ." "I delivered unto you first of all," wrote the greatest of His apostles, "that which also I received, how that Christ died for our sins according to the scriptures; and . . . was buried, and that he rose again the third day according to the scriptures." To depart from the principle that the Christian faith is neither a human philosophy, nor the offspring of a natural instinct, but a divine revelation, found, and found alone, in Holy Scripture, is to cut at the very root of the Gospel.'

Bishop Neill strongly objected to Poole-Connor's comments, his chief complaint being that he had ascribed to him views concerning co-operation with the Roman Church which, as a matter of fact (he said), he did not hold. Poole-Connor quoted the Bishop's words in full: '"I cannot imagine," he writes, "where you got the idea that I believe it possible to co-operate with the Church of Rome as she now is. I have so repeatedly and publicly maintained the contrary. The position for which I have stood is that the best service that we can render to the Church of Rome is to strengthen evangelical witness in predominantly Roman Catholic countries; this is very well known to my many friends in the Waldensian Church in Italy, and in Latin America." "You must admit," he continues in a second letter, "that it is a little hard for a man who has maintained for thirty-three years of public life an inflexible evangelical witness to be represented as advocating, of all things, co-operation with the Roman Church, as that Church now is."'

Poole-Connor responded: 'We confess that on reading these words we rubbed our eyes; we even changed our spectacles. Are there *two* Bishop Stephen Neills? we asked ourselves. If so, which one of them wrote a volume entitled *Christ and His Church*? For in the latter we read (p. 206), "The absence of Rome from all ecumenical discussions is greatly to be regretted; both because the other churches have less than full access to the great tradition of Roman wisdom and devotion, and because Rome herself can gain so much by association and co-operation on equal terms with Christians of other communions." In view of the Bishop's letter to us, are we to understand that while he advocates Rome's co-operation with other communions he cannot recommend other communions to co-operate with her? The situation is very confusing.

'We turn to page 107 for further guidance, but are not greatly helped. There, after a reference to Rome as "the greatest of all the churches", we find the Bishop saying: "It must not for a moment be supposed that the World Council of Churches" – of which until 1951 Bishop Neill was Associate General Secretary – "is being organised with any purpose of hostility to Rome. Nothing could be further from the truth. Membership of the World Council is open to any church which professes faith in Jesus Christ as God and Saviour. *The invitation to Rome stands always open" [italics ours]*. The Bishop wonders where we got our idea that he thought it possible to co-operate with Rome, as she now is. We fear that he will think us very dull; but we got the idea from such passages as those which we have just quoted.'

Poole-Connor was constantly at his post in cautioning about the destructive power of error. He had witnessed the collapse of evangelical Nonconformity, and could not bear to see the few remaining Bible-loving churches still largely unworried about their enemies. In the spring issue of the *Quarterly* (1958) he wrote: 'There are probably few of the cautionary Scriptures to which it behoves the Christian believer to give more attention than those which relate to teachers of error . . . In the sphere of religion changes of outlook are taking place which are little short of revolutionary; changes which the evangelical believer cannot but regard as fraught with the utmost spiritual peril.

'The growing insistence that all forms of separation on doctrinal grounds, not excluding that which brought about the Reformation, are sinful schism, is steadily reversing the attitude of the Protestant churches not only to the Church of Rome, but toward religious beliefs in general. Doctrines which in earlier years would have been regarded as the gravest of heresy are now accepted with scarcely the lift of an eyebrow. Meanwhile, the dazzling vision of "one church in one world" becomes ever clearer in outline; and the day seems not far distant when Babylon the Great, masking doctrinal confusion under external pomp and power, will again enter upon the stage of history in a new and perhaps final form.'

He wrote two booklets on the World Council of Churches. The first was, *The World Council of Churches' Cure for Disunity: Its Nature and Cost*. The headings were simple and the subject plainly expounded – 'The Malady as Seen by the WCC', 'The Remedy Proposed by the WCC', and 'The Price of the Proposed Remedy'. This was published by the ICCC. The second, *The WCC – Whence and Whither?* was issued by the British Evangelical Council.

Of well-known, leading ministers few took up and echoed his warnings in the same way as Dr Martyn Lloyd-Jones. Addressing a Bible League meeting, he made the point that when evangelicals worked side by side with those whom they knew did not take the evangelical view of scriptural inerrancy and authority, they were unconsciously not treating Scripture as the final authority. They claimed to accept the Bible as God's Word, and to acknowledge the authority of its definitions, yet they found no difficulty in publicly co-operating with men whose views contradicted their own; in some cases even with those who did not accept the atoning death of our Lord. They said, in effect, that Christian love and fellowship were more important than right views about the Scriptures and about the work of Christ on the cross.

However, in all the darkening gloom Poole-Connor was quick to recognise and encourage positive developments, an example of the latter coming in the late 1950s. In the autumn of 1958, he wrote of a new outlook which caused him to make a remarkable prophecy:

'The present theological outlook in the English-speaking world, viewed from the evangelical standpoint, is one of mingled light and shade. Some of its features call for much thankfulness, others can only be regarded with distress. Amongst the former is the remarkable revival of interest in what may broadly be termed Puritan theological literature. There are various evidences of this. It is the testimony of the Evangelical Library, whose branches now not only "run over the wall", but have begun to reach out to the ends of the earth, that the type of volume which is finding an increasingly eager welcome is that which presents the doctrines of the reformed faith in Puritan garb. Equally notable is the experience of the recently established Banner of Truth Trust, whose re-issue of works of this nature has met with a response beyond all expectation.

'It is our hope that this re-awakened interest in works that represent a warmer, a more reverential, and a more spiritually intelligent understanding of the Gospel, may herald a coming visitation of grace amongst the people of God, now so urgently needed. It is not infrequently one of the first evidences of a movement of God upon the soul that a man begins to turn to books that correspond to his new-born sense of need. May not this be now the case on a larger scale?'

Having been nurtured on the writings of the Puritans he knew their value. There followed in the succeeding issues of the *Bible League Quarterly* reviews of these books: 'They are all excellently printed and bound and present Puritan theology in its most powerful form. Taken as a whole, they are characterised by a depth, a clarity and a force that renders them of the utmost value.'

His attitude towards election and predestination comes out very clearly in his enthusiastic review of a new volume of Spurgeon's *Revival Year Sermons* (*Bible League Quarterly,* summer 1959): 'It is our personal judgement that Spurgeon throughout his ministry maintained a truer balance between the doctrines of divine sovereignty and human responsibility than did many both before and after him. He was a firm believer in the Five Points of Calvinism; he preached them without apology or diminution; he regarded them indeed as central to the Gospel, yet he saw that it was a doctrine that could be sorely abused. He saw, too, that there were other doctrines taught in Scripture complementary to the Five Points no less divinely inspired. The volume will well repay a study of those who are earnestly desiring to witness another visitation of grace such as that which blessed the British Isles in the years of Spurgeon's prime.'

Poole-Connor described himself as a Calvinist; however, he did not hold all the Five Points of Calvinism. He did not accept particular redemption, and in this respect he followed men like J. C. Ryle. In *Evangelicalism in England*, he deals with the matter in detail (pp. 172-5), and draws attention to the vital difference between the systems of Arminius and Calvin. He had a mind that was too logical and deep to treat the subject superficially. It is abundantly clear that in general he embraced the position taken by the reformed confessions of faith on the disputed points.

Perhaps even more significant is Poole-Connor's view of John Wesley's position, quoted from Fletcher of Madeley, 'He *[Wesley]* is not an Arminian ... for he constantly maintains that man is only free to do evil.' Poole-Connor used the word Methodist rather than Arminian, saying, 'Methodism does not share the Pelagian* sympathies of Arminianism. It takes a darker view of original sin as more than a disease, as *complete* depravity *[italics mine – DGF]*. It attributes human freedom since the Fall not to any partial survival of original freedom, but to the direct prevenient grace of the Spirit of God in the individual soul. And it lays far greater stress upon definite conversion and regeneration as a necessary subjective experience for every man.' [1]

In drawing up the confession of faith of the FIEC, he was careful not to exclude the Wesleyan, but he did in fact exclude the thorough-going Arminian. The relevant article reads: 'The utter depravity of human nature in consequence of the Fall and the necessity for regeneration.' He also saw that there was a danger of

---

*Pelagius, an English monk, joined with Celestius circa AD 400 to deny original sin and affirm man's freedom to do good or evil. He held that salvation is therefore by works, while acknowledging that divine grace helps. He was strongly opposed by Augustine.

emphasising election too much, and did take occasion to warn against this in the *Bible League Quarterly*. However, he considered the 'recent revival of Calvinism . . . a matter for sincere thankful-ness'. His own attitude towards the sovereignty of God was best seen in his attitude towards revival. For him it was a visitation of grace.

Poole-Connor had been personally involved in the founding of the Evangelical Library – one of the first new agencies for the promotion of Puritan literature in 20th-century Britain. In 1942 he had visited the infant Library, then called the 'Beddington Free Grace Library', started by a Christian businessman, Geoffrey Williams. Together with Dr Martyn Lloyd-Jones he had come to the conclusion that this 'storehouse of evangelical truth' should be brought to London. He was involved even at a practical level in the transfer of the books and the erection of the shelves.

The place Poole-Connor had in the inception of the Library is best described by the words of its President, Dr Lloyd-Jones: 'I have often spoken of what Mr Poole-Connor meant to us, especially in the early years. I shall never forget as long as I live when we met in the temporary place we had in Gloucester Road. I am quite certain that were it not for his enthusiasm, and his unfailing optimism, we might very well have floundered at this point, but he would not be discouraged. He was so certain of the future of this Library that he persuaded us all to continue. Above all, he was such a gracious man, a man who read very widely, and a man of wisdom and under-standing.' Geoffrey Williams, the founder and Secretary of the Library, paid a tribute to his graciousness, 'His crowning ability was his extraordinary gift whereby he inspired a spirit of harmony, and which by a word or even a look, could banish the very thought of discord, calm the rising of troubled waters, and cause the scent of love's precious ointment to pervade every company amongst which he was numbered.'

In taking delight in, and encouraging, Puritan and Calvinistic literature, Poole-Connor was not unaware of C. H. Spurgeon's prophetic words concerning its revival. In 1871 Calvinism was widely regarded as defunct. In that year Professor Froude, of Oxford, had declared to the students of St. Andrews: 'Everyone here present must have become familiar in late years with the change of tone throughout Europe and America on the subject of Calvinism. After being accepted for two centuries in all Protestant countries, it has come to be regarded by liberal thinkers as a system of belief incredible in itself, dishonouring to its object, and as intolerable as it has been itself intolerant.' In 1873 Dr Dale also had described Calvinism as obsolete. Spurgeon replied to Dale in the following terms: 'Those who labour to smother "Calvinism" will find that it dies hard, and, it may be, they will come forward, after many defeats, to perceive the certain fact that it will outlive its opponents. Its funeral oration has been pronounced many times before now, but the performance has been premature. It will live when the present phase of religious misbelief has gone down to eternal execration amid the groans of those whom it has undone. Today it may be sneered at; nevertheless, it is but yesterday that it numbered among its adherents the ablest men of the age; and tomorrow it may be, when once again there shall be giants in theology, it will come to the front, and ask in vain for its adversaries.'

Poole-Connor's discerning stewardship of the editorial influence of the *Bible League Quarterly* never flagged. In the spring issue of 1960, he drew attention to the Barthianism that appeared in an article in *The Christian*: 'The writer says, "Perhaps the most serious heterodoxy is to read the Bible as a textbook, or a quarry for sermons, or as an argument against opponents of one's view, or as a source book for some academic thesis, or as a means of comfort, instead of the trysting place in which to meet God." We can only say that if to use the Word of God in the manner described is a major heresy, it is one of which our Lord and His apostles were all guilty. It was supremely their "textbook", repeatedly quoted as the authority for their teaching and their correction of error; they instructed ministers to make it the "quarry" for their preaching, and believers to turn to it for comfort; the latter being one of the purposes, they said, for which aforetime it was written. That God does apply His Word at times to the individual soul is blessedly true; but that does not cancel out *2 Timothy 3.16.*'

In 1961 the *New English Bible* was published, and in the winter edition of the *Quarterly*, when reviewing a specimen page that had appeared in the *Telegraph,* he expressed distress at the way the atonement was explained away. He dealt with texts in a scholarly way, and in closing remarked, 'If this is the manner in which the new version is to explain away the essential nature of our Lord's atonement, we tremble for the consequences of its circulation.'

Poole-Connor felt an increasing loneliness toward the end of his life, not simply because, with advancing age, he was losing his old acquaintances, but more on account of the severe criticism he received for his analysis of the evangelical situation outside his own circle. The spiritual climate was against him. When conditions decline spiritually, people become complacent and less conscious of the changes that take place. It would seem that he should have borne the name Jeremiah, rather than Joshua. Dr Lloyd-Jones certainly appreciated his ministry as Editor of the *Bible League Quarterly*, saying:

'He was concerned about the propagation of the Truth and the defence of the Truth. He was a man who had the keenest discriminations. He was one of the finest reviewers of books I have ever read. He had a capacity for not only seeing the excellence of a book, but what was left out. There have been men in the last twenty years who have been lauded as evangelicals, but they were not evangelicals for Mr Poole-Connor. You have got to watch what a man does not say, and then you frequently discover that your great evangelical is not an evangelical at all.

'He was not the sort of man who just praised everybody, and whose idea of a saint was that one should be more or less spineless and just affable, pleasant and nice. He conformed to the New Testament pattern. He did not want to enter into controversy, but you have to do this when the Truth is being hidden. The New Testament is a very polemical document. He exposed and denounced error because he so loved the Truth and felt that it was essential that this should be done. But his spirit was always so sweet and gentle. He always gave the impression that he regretted having to do this. It has been said that he was contentious, but criticisms generally tell us much more about the critic than they do about the man criticised. His whole method and mode of controversy was thoroughly Christian. May God grant us more such critics and leaders in these flabby, sentimental days, in which, unfortunately, we live.'

Shortly before his death, Poole-Connor spoke at an FIEC regional meeting, and described the situation as he saw it. He used the illustration of a ship going into harbour, and the red and green lights which could be seen, warning of danger, and beckoning towards a safe path. When referring to warning lights he spoke of the general increase of Barthianism. He explained very carefully what this was, and how it was increasing. He also gave a warning against the *New English Bible*. When he came to 'beckoning lights', he spoke of the publication of Puritan literature by the Banner of Truth. 'There was no finer era of preaching than the Puritan era,' he said. He warmly recommended such books. He referred them to revival, and the hope he cherished of one day seeing it for himself.

After the meeting, at the tea table, a person expressed surprise that he had not referred to the Billy Graham campaigns as a 'beckoning light', and asked him what he thought of them. He replied, 'I say with the apostle Paul, that I rejoice that Christ is preached.' The enquirer felt that there was some qualification in his words, and asked him if there was anything he took exception to. Poole-Connor said that he was not happy about those who shared the platform with Billy Graham. His friend quickly protested that this policy gave those who were not evangelical an opportunity to hear the Gospel. He replied that, for those who were at the meeting, it would seem that since Billy Graham and men of opposite views shared in the same service, either the differences were not very great, or that they could not really matter.

In 1955 he had referred to Billy Graham as a man raised up of God to preach the Gospel to the multitudes, and his campaigns as a movement of the Spirit. Had he since adopted an unnecessarily pessimistic view of the situation? Had Poole-Connor changed? The outstanding characteristic about him was his steadfastness. He was utterly true and unswerving to the end. It was Billy Graham who had changed, and with him many others on both sides of the Atlantic. The 'new evangelicalism' that had arisen was a departure from the old. It stood for 'infiltration' and not 'separation'.

In April, 1951, Billy Graham had written, 'We do not condone, nor have fellowship with any form of modernism.' In the following year he said, 'We have never had a modernist on our Executive Committee,' and 'The modernists do not support us anywhere.' Subsequently, however, he went so far as to co-operate even with the Church of Rome.

Poole-Connor could never understand how Billy Graham could send converts from Catholic backgrounds back to their own churches where they would not hear the Gospel, but instead have their newly-found faith undermined. The change in Billy Graham epitomises the radical change of attitude on the part of evangelicals towards those who in former days were seen as the 'enemies of the cross of Christ'.

In spite of his sense of loneliness, and the increasing decline, Poole-Connor was ever a man of faith, convinced that God would eventually send a visitation of grace. His message at the FIEC Assembly at Cardiff in 1957, on the subject of 'revival', will never be forgotten by those present. Some consider that it was the greatest moment in his life. This godly man of eighty-five was given a remarkable degree of spiritual power, which was felt by everyone there. He knew what revival really was. He told the assembled company that when he was called to the pastorate of Talbot Tabernacle, he had the closest possible fellowship with his predecessor Frank Henry White during the remaining two years of his life. 'Frank Henry White was one whom God mightily used in what we commonly call the 1859 Revival, and I used to go and sit at his feet and hear him telling story after story of what he himself had witnessed, and scenes in which he himself had taken part, so that I have a very clear conception of what true revival really means.' He was a link with a day that had known the 'goings of the Son of Man' – the victorious marches of Christ through the land, capturing vast numbers of souls to Himself. He had a yardstick with which to measure the times. His booklet, *Visitations of Grace,* expressed his intense longing that God would grant 'seasons of refreshing'.

This desire for revival had been in his heart for many years, ever since he read of the revival in New England under Jonathan Edwards in the 18th century. He did all he could to prepare the way for just such a time, but he did not live to see it. Since then, the subject of revival has often been addressed by others. Some have gone as far as to point out that the Spirit has perhaps been grieved through compromise, but the majority have not accepted such a possibility.

As the moral and spiritual condition of the country continued to decline, Poole-Connor felt strongly that the introduction of the television into so many homes had been the means of familiarising people with many things that defiled them. The accelerated collapse into the 'new morality' in the 1960s was not far ahead.

Poole-Connor was to leave behind him nearly 300 churches that were true to the principles for which he stood, not to mention many churches and individuals who had been helped by his printed ministry to remain faithful. Yet he claimed neither thought nor credit for himself. Indeed, he felt he had accomplished very little. A short extract from his diary reads, 'My spiritual activities over a long course of years, preaching, teaching, lecturing, writing, have left no permanent mark on my generation, and a new body of younger men have risen up that "know not Joseph". How little – and *how little* – there is to show for a lifetime's labour. Yet I have sought to do God's will day by day, and to do His work faithfully. Noted that with Jacob's entry upon his new stage of spiritual life he was lamed. The "Prince with God" "halted upon his thigh". So Paul with "Third Heaven" visions, was given a "thorn in the flesh". There is no escape from this!'

His sense of ineffectiveness rose from deep-seated humility, but there was unquestionably a lack of appreciation shown to him by the wider Christian community, and here the parallel with Spurgeon is very marked. He was certainly a God-given leader and banner-bearer, and the fact that few were willing to be led does not detract from his greatness. He set his course by the Word of God, and pursued it faithfully to the end. He was a man who 'had understanding of the times, and knew what Israel ought to do'.

He entered St. James' Hospital, Balham, with an infected prostate gland on December 5th, 1961, returning to his home at Streatham just after Christmas. He seemed somewhat improved and brighter. He dictated some notes to his wife of thoughts that had occurred to him during his illness, hoping to speak from them:

'1. How varied are the experiences of God's people – sick, imprisoned, naked.

2. In all these experiences our Lord is one with His people – sick

with them, naked with them, in prison with them, even though He Himself was never sick or in prison.

3. Here, therefore, is an opportunity of ministering to Him, even to the least of His brethren.

4. Here are the marks of God's elect, for whom a kingdom has been prepared before the foundation of the world.

5. Here, too, are the marks of having passed from death unto life. "We know that we have passed from death unto life, because we love the brethren." '

Aged and dying, the activity of his mind reflected his desire to use his last ounce of strength in fulfilling the calling given to him, namely, to meet the spiritual needs of others. It was the first time in his life that he had been ill. A close friend visited him shortly before his death. Poole-Connor held his hand for twenty minutes, and said to him, 'Don't be distressed if you see me in pain. It is purely physical suffering – my faith is stronger than it ever was.' On January 20th, 1962, God called home this faithful servant. He had fought a good fight, he had finished his course. So he passed over, and all the trumpets sounded for him on the other side.

A funeral service was held at Lansdowne Evangelical Free Church, West Norwood, London and a great company was present. His earthly remains were buried in West Norwood Cemetery, not far from those of C. H. Spurgeon, whose example meant so much to him. Shortly afterwards a memorial service was held at Westminster Chapel. On both occasions tributes were paid to him by men who had witnessed at close hand his great instrumentality in God's service, and the saintliness of his life.

The Rev H. Brash Bonsall later recalled that as the hushed company left the impressive memorial service at Westminster Chapel, he talked with Mrs Poole-Connor. During the service some had remarked on the number of years they had known him. She said to him softly, and with great emphasis, 'But I have known him longer than them all. I have known him for seventy-five years.'

Edith was a wonderful life partner for him. He could never have accomplished all that he did were it not for her. She held all his convictions, and supported him in every way. They bore together all the burdens of his multi-faceted ministry. She was the proof-reader of his prodigious literary output, and of course, they read the Scriptures and prayed together every day. Their happy and har-monious married life was an example to all. Mrs Poole-Connor was wonderfully sustained during the time of her bereavement. She told her family and friends that the separation would only be for a few weeks. It was as though she was referring to a railway journey, and her husband was waiting for her at the end. In God's wisdom the expected few weeks were lengthened out into more than three years, before she went to be with Christ. Her own explanation of this longer period was that she had relied so greatly upon her husband that the Lord had given her this period to teach her to lean on Him alone. And during this period she was able to tell the writer, with great clarity, many important facts about her husband's activities and convictions. She had reached the age of ninety-five, before crossing the 'river' very peacefully.

Notes

1   W. A. Curtis, *History of Creeds and Confessions of Faith*, T. & T. Clark, Edinburgh, 1911, p. 332.

12

A Biographer's Afterthoughts
2004

THE MOST striking feature of the life of Poole-Connor was his consistency. As his convictions grew he not only expressed them openly, but acted upon them and remained consistent in them. The great historian, G. M. Trevelyan commended William Wilberforce 'for his complete honesty of purpose' in his efforts to abolish slavery, saying, 'With his talents and position he would probably have been Pitt's successor as Prime Minister, if he had preferred party to mankind. His sacrifice of one kind of fame and power gave him another and a nobler title to remembrance.'[1] In like manner, Poole-Connor could undoubtedly have made a far greater name for himself in the Christian world had he concealed his views or merely stated them, without acting on them. He did not accept the situation as he found it, and accommodate himself to it. His whole life was a faithful commentary on his great passion for the preservation of authentic evangelicalism, and the unity and well-being of God's faithful people.

The space of over forty years since his death has given us time to see the way in which church life in the UK has developed, particularly with the Fellowship of churches he founded. The general apostasy about which he so strongly warned has continued, so that now evangelicalism barely exists within the historic Nonconformist denominations. For a time, thankfully, more voices were raised than during Poole-Connor's lifetime to oppose modernism and liberalism. The ministry of Dr Martyn Lloyd-Jones, for example, clearly supplemented Poole-Connor's in providing a powerful call to separation from those who denied the fundamentals of the faith.

Poole-Connor's Fellowship of Independent Evangelical Churches has certainly grown in *numbers* of churches, the 300 at the founder's death rising to around 420 today. Forty years ago it was expected that it would grow very considerably larger. Ominously, perhaps, the Fellowship has also grown in its organisational structure. From the very beginning its council assumed powers that many believed belonged solely to the local church, such as the accreditation of ministers, and the linking of its member churches with other groups via membership of the British Evangelical Council. (The latter decision was made by the council acting alone.) However, the process of increasingly complex organisational development continued apace after Poole-Connor's death, with the adoption of a new constitution and other decisions. The relatively loose Fellowship of consenting churches of the earliest days has seen the increase of 'centralised power'.

Furthermore, the question must be asked, is the Fellowship *united* and *free of error*, as Poole-Connor envisaged? He had hoped that it would be enough to require churches to sign annually an evangelical basis of faith. But do all the member churches really believe the first article of the Declaration of Faith which defends the exclusive sufficiency of the Word of God? Or are there churches that believe that God still speaks directly through prophecy, implying that the Bible is not enough? Sadly, there are many such churches within the FIEC, holding a charismatic view of ongoing revelation. Poole-Connor believed in the cessation of the miraculous gifts, and would unquestionably be horrified at the large number of churches within the Fellowship that believe to the contrary.

He would also be horrified at the modern worship scene. In chapter nine reference is made to his pamphlet entitled, *Take These Things Hence.* He was concerned about the fact that 'theatricals and Passion Plays' were 'commonplace in so-called evangelical parishes'. He objected to Christians attending the theatre, and especially to the theatre being brought into the church. The use of drama in Fellowship churches in 'worship' services would also amaze him. He would certainly be greatly disturbed to observe the behaviour of some prominent men within the Fellowship with regard to the Church of Rome, for he was an unashamed Protestant and would (in his own turn of phrase) 'rub his eyes and change his spectacles' on reading of those who have indicated their recognition of that apostate body, the Church of Rome, as a true church of Jesus Christ.

It must be kept in mind that Poole-Connor did not live to see the arrival of the new group of spiritual dangers that emerged in the 1960s and 1970s, and there is good reason to believe that these may have greatly altered his vision for evangelical unity. The churches he drew together were untainted by such things as charismatic ways, contemporary Christian worship, openness to new evangelicalism and even Rome. Therefore, the FIEC as originally conceived had no machinery for discipline. Had he foreseen such phenomena, he may well have proposed much tighter rules for admission to, and remaining in, the Fellowship.

Today, Poole-Connor would find it difficult to believe that the FIEC is the same body that he founded. The recent move to make an alliance with evangelical Anglicans through the short-lived movement 'Essentially Evangelical' was a clear denial of the original position of the FIEC and Poole-Connor's view of second-degree separation. There is no doubt that he did not believe we should have public fellowship with churches that were still in compromised denominations. More recently the British Evangelical Council has assumed a new name, 'Affinity', and abandoned separation from churches that belong to and support unsound denominations. The Fellowship is the largest constituent member of that Council. Thus the original vision and intention of Poole-Connor has been swept aside.

Many of the churches which have joined the Fellowship over the years are 'Independents' in the full sense of the word, believing in the autonomy of the local church in all matters of government and discipline. Their liberty enables each one to separate from those in error, and to have fellowship with those that are sound in the faith. An *organised* bond is certainly not necessary, and may well bind such churches to those who depart from the faith or engage in dangerous practices. Because the earlier Fellowship churches were untouched by such problems, Poole-Connor did not recognise this danger, and it may well be said, with hindsight, that true Independency would have served his purpose better.

The New Testament, after all, knows only two 'churches' – the local, autonomous church, and the church of all the redeemed of all ages. Nowhere do we find an organised fellowship group in any region of the New Testament lands. In *Revelation* chapters 2 and 3 no visible organisation united the seven churches. No mechanism existed to bring them together to deal with local problems. Each 'candlestick' *(KJV)* is a separate congregation in direct association with its Head, looking to Christ alone for its strength. We should not really talk about the 'early *church*' (singular), but of 'early *churches*'. The concept of a 'large, united, powerful *church*' lying behind the vision of the FIEC can now be seen to have been misconceived. Poole-Connor's earnest desire that all sound churches should be separated from unfaithful churches, and united in heart with those that were truly biblical, was noble and right, but the *way* he sought to implement that unity has fallen foul of the declining standards in evangelical life since his homecall. Nevertheless, his clear views on separation, and his desire for real fellowship between the faithful, still has so much to teach us.

Notes

1   G. M. Trevelyan, *English Social History*, The Reprint Society, 1948.

Appendix
Dr D. Martyn Lloyd-Jones and Separatism

THE NAME OF Dr Martyn Lloyd-Jones is often mentioned in connection with the promotion of evangelical unity. His reaction to the present situation in the FIEC would probably have similarities to that which we have supposed for Poole-Connor. His views on separation would make him strongly opposed to the quest for organised association with evangelical Anglicans. He had reservations about the FIEC very early on, seeing that there was a danger of making a body that would take powers from the local church. He held, for instance, that it was wrong to organise a religious body to act as Trustees for a local church. He also believed without doubt in so-called second-degree separation.

The author was at the very meeting of the former Puritan Conference committee in 1970 when it was decided to bring the Conference to an end. Dr Lloyd-Jones called this committee meeting, at which he emphatically proposed that the Puritan Conference should come to an end because Dr J. I. Packer, a member, was involved with false teachers, as demonstrated by his book, *Growing into Union*. J. I. Packer was clearly still an evangelical, but was co-operating closely with men who denied evangelical doctrines. Dr Lloyd-Jones put into concrete form the committee's belief in second-degree separation. He and Poole-Connor were of one mind on this matter, as were many others.

Postscript
Is the 'Formula' Still Workable?
Dr Peter Masters

BEFORE HIS homecall in 2004, my long-standing friend, David G. Fountain, asked if I would add a postscript to the reissue of this biography – a book that captivated me at its first publication in 1966. The life of E. J. Poole-Connor made a great impact on me at the time, especially his lifelong intensity of commitment to the service of Christ, so that he never retired, maintaining a deeply significant ministry to the very end.

I would like to amplify what I believe is a crucial point for today, which applies to evangelicalism world-wide, wherever God's people seek to express fellowship with those of like faith. It concerns the formula for unity between churches.

The wider work of E. J. Poole-Connor fell into two parts, firstly the call for evangelicals to separate from doctrinally mixed denominations and organisations, and secondly the call to express evangelical unity between individual congregations. To achieve the second of these, he set forward the strikingly simple formula, that evangelicals should unite on the basis of *essentials*, laying aside *non-essentials*. Essentials he defined as the vital, central doctrines of the Word, whereas non-essentials were matters such as the method of baptism and church government. These, he believed, would continue to be important to individual churches, but should not obstruct inter-church fellowship. (Despite his own views, Calvinism and Arminianism seem to have been regarded as non-essentials.)

This formula – 'essentials, not non-essentials' – was well received by many people, and has been much quoted over the years. Dr Martyn Lloyd-Jones became a notable advocate of this policy. However, the question must be asked – is it sufficient for today?

In the decade following Poole-Connor's death a host of new problems came on the scene which seriously challenged the usefulness of the policy. The formula had focused on what churches *believed*, and appeared very workable in the days when most evangelical churches *practised* the same kind of worship and Christian life. But after Poole-Connor's death marked differences in *practice* came into the churches, such as contemporary, entertainment-style worship, drama, and charismatic signs and prophecies. These activities seriously challenged spiritual, reverent worship. They also brought the world into the church and, in the case of charismatic prophecy, undermined the exclusive authority of Scripture.

What churches actually *do* suddenly became as important as what they *believe*, because what churches *practise* could change their character completely. The simple formula – 'essentials, not non-essentials' – now became a danger to 'traditional' evangelical churches, because it bound them together with churches of very different practice and outlook. Churches are united by this formula undertake not to make an issue of 'non-essentials', for this would be divisive. Harmful practices, therefore, go unchallenged, and bad activities permeate the whole group. This is exactly what has happened in the UK in recent years within the FIEC (and also in most regional associations of Grace Baptist churches). The practices of new evangelicalism have entered unchallenged, in time taking over the majority of member churches, and in the case of modern entertainment-style worship, dominating the major annual 'assembly' of the Fellowship. Activities once considered offensive and unbiblical have stolen away hearts. It comes through very clearly in this biography that Poole-Connor would have been a very strong opponent of these developments. It is certainly a tragedy in the years following his death, as new decadent trends emerged, there was no one of his stature to reassess the formula for unity.

Even where churches relate together on a baptistic and Calvinistic basis (a number of such groups having come into being in the USA), this point is still vital – is the basis of fellowship solely doctrinal, or does it include practices? It would certainly appear that Satan's strategy today is to corrupt churches by harmful activities, as well as by harmful teachings, and we ignore this at our peril. This writer agrees entirely with the author that in such wayward times the best solution for unity is historic Independency, where churches have liberty to relate or not to relate with other churches. But whether we are independent, or those who desire some more organised form of association, to disregard unbiblical practices will lead to ever-deepening trouble. It may well be, for example, that Satan's plan to make Rome acceptable to evangelicals is not the route of doctrinal compromise (at least, not yet) but by the standardisation of contemporary Christian worship, charismatic practice, and similar trends. After all, if he can persuade all to worship and act in the same way, all will soon 'feel' they are the same.

A solemn warning may be gleaned from Poole-Connor's account of the collapse of evangelicalism in the denominations. As this book shows, the three main Nonconformist denominations constituted the largest number of worshippers in England in the 1870s, at which time they were almost entirely soundly evangelical. Yet by the 1950s, few evangelicals remained in them (and now there are almost none). The reason is clear – stalwart Bible-lovers would not take a stand and defend the Truth when higher criticism came in, and thus they sold out the cause. They put unity before Truth. The parallel today in the area of *practice* is obvious. If evangelicals today put unity before corrupting practices, they too may lose virtually everything they have, with worldliness, flippancy, and low views of Scripture taking over hundreds more churches. This is the fatal flaw in the new 'Affinity' alliance (formerly the British Evangelical Council). It is founded on the unity formula 'essentials not non-essentials' which lost its credibility forty years ago. 'Affinity' will inevitably result in the worst practices represented in affiliated churches permeating the entire body.

May God stir the hearts of pastors and leaders who see the danger to speak out against the tide of unbiblical practices. The words of Abraham Kuyper speak to our present situation: 'When principles that run against your deepest convictions begin to win the day, then battle is your calling, and peace has become sin; you must, at the price of dearest peace, lay your convictions bare before friend and enemy, with all the fire of your faith.'